China's Arms Acqu

A Quest for 'Superb and Secret Weapons'

Stockholm International Peace Research Institute

SIPRI is an independent international institute for research into problems of peace and conflict, especially those of arms control and disarmament. It was established in 1966 to commemorate Sweden's 150 years of unbroken peace.

The Institute is financed mainly by the Swedish Parliament. The staff and the Governing Board are international. The Institute also has an Advisory Committee as an international consultative body.

The Governing Board is not responsible for the views expressed in the publications of the Institute.

sipri

Stockholm International Peace Research Institute

Frösunda, S-171 53 Solna, Sweden
Cable: SIPRI
Telephone: 46 8/655 97 00
Telefax: 46 8/655 97 33
E-mail: sipri@sipri.se
Internet URL: http://www.sipri.se

China's Arms Acquisitions from Abroad

A Quest for 'Superb and Secret Weapons'

SIPRI Research Report No. 11

Bates Gill and Taeho Kim

OXFORD UNIVERSITY PRESS
1995

Oxford University Press, Walton Street, Oxford OX2 6DP

Oxford New York
Athens Auckland Bangkok Bombay
Calcutta Cape Town Dar es Salaam Delhi
Florence Hong Kong Istanbul Karachi
Kuala Lumpur Madras Madrid Melbourne
Mexico City Nairobi Paris Singapore
Taipei Tokyo Toronto
and associated companies in
Berlin Ibadan

Oxford is a trade mark of Oxford University Press

Published in the United States
by Oxford University Press Inc., New York

© SIPRI 1995

British Library Cataloguing in Publication Data
Data available

Library of Congress Cataloging-in-Publication Data
Data available

ISBN 0–19–829195–7
ISBN 0–19–829196–5 (pbk.)

Typeset and originated by Stockholm International Peace Research Institute
Printed in Great Britain on acid-free paper by
Biddles Ltd., Guildford and King's Lynn

Contents

Preface

At the dawn of the 'Pacific Century', as China grows stronger and seeks to play a greater role in regional and world affairs, it will be important for the international community to understand the capabilities and intentions of the Chinese leadership in all spheres, not only security-related matters. With its concern to shed light on important questions of global and regional peace and security, SIPRI offers this volume as a contribution to this process.

The co-authors are well-suited professionally to the task. Dr Bates Gill, head of the SIPRI Project on Security and Arms Control in East Asia, has studied Chinese arms trade and production since the mid-1980s, work which has included frequent research visits to China as well as two year-long stays on the mainland. Dr Taeho Kim, a Visiting Scholar and Research Associate at the Mershon Center for Public Affairs at Ohio State University in 1993–95, has returned to his post as senior China analyst in the Policy Planning Directorate at the Korea Institute for Defence Analyses in Seoul, Republic of Korea. Their command of the Chinese language and access to extensive resources in their respective institutes, their experience and contacts in China, and their many years of monitoring China combine to present a comprehensive and in-depth examination of Chinese arms acquisitions from abroad.

The authors conclude that China's historical search abroad for the means to modernize its arsenal has been problematic and only partially successful. Indeed, historical legacies will continue to weigh heavily as constraints on current and future efforts to modernize China's military through the acquisition of foreign weapons and military technologies. Nevertheless, because of and in spite of these constraints, China will continue to vigorously pursue its military modernization effort, and this effort will include the quest for arms and technologies from abroad. However, as the Chinese themselves well recognize, this path to military modernization will be slow and difficult.

SIPRI is pleased to support this effort initiated by the Project on Security and Arms Control in East Asia. In addition to this study, the Project has published research on the prospects for multilateral and bilateral security dialogue in North-East Asia and on conventional arms trade, production and control in East Asia. The work of the Project has benefited enormously from collaboration with the SIPRI Project on Arms Transfers and the SIPRI Project on Arms Production.

Adam Daniel Rotfeld
Director of SIPRI
August 1995

Acknowledgements

This research report would not have been possible without the assistance of numerous persons and institutions at various stages of its preparation. The study emerged from research we presented to the Fifth Staunton Hill Conference on the People's Liberation Army (PLA), sponsored by the American Enterprise Institute and convened at Staunton Hill, Virginia, USA, in June 1994. The conference brought together academics, officials, researchers and journalists specializing in the Chinese military and held an extensive but focused discussion on various aspects of the PLA. We are grateful to the conference organizers and participants and wish to thank the conference host and former US Ambassador to China, James R. Lilley.

Several conference participants later reviewed the manuscript at its various stages. We remain indebted to their work on the Chinese military in general and to their invaluably helpful comments on the manuscript in particular. They are Tai Ming Cheung, John Frankenstein, Paul H. B. Godwin, Alexander C. Huang and David Shambaugh. In addition, we express our appreciation to colleagues at SIPRI for their extensive and insightful suggestions with regard to the arms trade and weapon technologies—Eric Arnett, Ravinder Pal Singh, Pieter Wezeman and Siemon Wezeman—and to the Leaders of the SIPRI Arms Transfers and Arms Production projects—Ian Anthony and Elisabeth Sköns, respectively—for the project data they provided for this report. Our editors, Peter Rea and Connie Wall, especially deserve our heartfelt praise and gratitude for their perception, devotion to detail and professional encouragement. Cynthia Loo, Project Secretary at SIPRI, unfailingly provided her assistance in numerous ways.

The Stockholm International Peace Research Institute and the Mershon Center at Ohio State University provided us with excellent research environments and warm hospitality. Without the encouragement and support of their directors, Adam Daniel Rotfeld and Charles F. Hermann, respectively, our research would have been much less productive and enjoyable than was the case.

We note that the views expressed in the book are our own and do not represent the positions of any organizations with which we are affiliated.

Bates Gill
Stockholm, Sweden
Taeho Kim
Seoul, Republic of Korea

August 1995

Acronyms

AAM	Air-to-air missile
ACDA	(US) Arms Control and Disarmament Agency
AEW	Airborne early warning
AIFV	Armoured infantry fighting vehicle
ASEAN	Association of South-East Asian Nations
ASW	Anti-submarine warfare
ATBM	Anti-tactical ballistic missile
ATM	Anti-tank missile
AVIC	Aviation Industries of China
CAC	Chengdu Aircraft Industrial Corporation
CAREC	China National Aeroengine Corporation
CATIC	China Aero Technology Import–Export Corporation
CBM	Confidence-building measure
CC	Central Committee
CCP	Chinese Communist Party
CGE	Central government expenditure
CITIC	China International Trust and Investment Corporation
CKD	Component knocked down
CMC	Central Military Commission
CNAEC	China National Airborne Equipment Corporation
COCOM	Co-ordinating Committee (on Multilateral Export Controls)
COSTIND	Commission on Science, Technology and Industry for National Defence
CPSU	Communist Party of the Soviet Union
CPV	Chinese People's Volunteers
ELINT	Electronic intelligence
EW	Electronic warfare
FMS	Foreign Military Sales
GMD	Guomindang
GNP	Gross national product
GSD	General Staff Department of the PLA
HAMC	Harbin Aircraft Manufacturing Corporation
HUD	Head-up-display
HUDWAC	Head-up-display/weapon aiming computer

IAI	Israel Aircraft Industries
IFV	Infantry fighting vehicle
LETI	Leihua Electronics Technology Institute
MBI	Machine Building Industry
MBT	Main battle tank
MCBM	Military confidence-building measure
MFN	Most favoured nation
MIRV	Multiple independently targetable re-entry vehicle
MLRS	Multiple launch rocket system
MTCR	Missile Technology Control Regime
MTU	Motoren und Turbinen Union
NDIO	National Defence Industry Office
NDSTC	National Defence Science and Technology Commission
NORINCO	China North Industries Group
PAC	Pakistan Aeronautical Complex
PLA	People's Liberation Army
PLAAF	People's Liberation Army Air Force
PLAN	People's Liberation Army Navy
Poly	Poly Technologies Company
PPP	Purchasing power parity
PRC	People's Republic of China
R&D	Research and development
RAF	(British) Royal Air Force
Rmb	Renminbi
RRU	Rapid reaction unit
SAC	Shenyang Aircraft Corporation
SC	State Council
SEZ	Special Economic Zone
SIBAT	(Israeli) Foreign Defence Assistance and Defence Export (department)
SLOC	Sea lanes of communication
XAC	Xian Aircraft Corporation

1. Introduction: an old issue in new times

Thus we should seize the opportunity . . . to make a substantial study of all kinds of foreign machines and weapons in order to learn their secret completely. In times of disturbance they can be used to oppose aggression, and in times of peace they can show our prestige . . . After the battalions at the capital have learned to use these superb and secret weapons, learning to make them can be extended . . . (Li Hongzhang, Qing Dynasty official, 1863.[1])

I. Introduction

A study of Chinese arms acquisitions from abroad will shed light on a range of security-related issues—from the prospects for Chinese military modernization, to China's likely military posture in East Asia, to the strategic nature of China's role within that region. This research report seeks to broaden understanding in these areas by considering the following questions.

1. What are the past, present and likely future extent and nature of China's arms and military technology imports?
2. What do these acquisitions reveal about China's capabilities and intentions towards its neighbours in the East Asian region?
3. What impact will China's capabilities and intentions have on regional security?

In addressing these questions, the study seeks to go beyond tendentious analysis of China's military build-up by incorporating China's 150-year-long defence industry modernization effort up to the early 1990s and by assessing the problems and prospects for future Chinese arms acquisition policy. A number of constraints—historical, political, economic and technical—weigh heavily upon China's current and future arms imports in a way that limits the contribution of foreign acquisitions to Chinese military modernization, even as new sources of more advanced weapons and technology become available. As a result, China's military modernization through weapons and technol-

[1] Quoted in Teng, S.-Y. and Fairbank, J. K., *China's Response to the West: A Documentary Survey, 1839–1923* (Atheneum: New York, 1975), p. 73.

ogy imports will continue to be a slow and frustrating process. Para-doxically, closing the gap between Chinese aspirations and Chinese capabilities will both drive and constrain the foreign arms and tech-nology acquisition process.

II. Preliminary assessments

An enduring conundrum

At the heart of this subject lies an enduring conundrum. For more than 150 years Chinese leaders have recognized the need for military mod-ernization through the procurement and integration of foreign weapons and weapon technologies. Yet, for reasons which are strikingly persistent over time, China has been only partially suc-cessful in translating this procurement into a sustained indigenous capacity to develop and produce sophisticated weapons. This has often placed China in a weak position relative to its potential adversaries, further demonstrating the need for military modernization through arms imports.

This Chinese dilemma may be explained in part with reference to an abiding historical theme given voice during the last half of the 19th century in the now famous phrase of Qing Dynasty official Zhang Zhidong: *zhongxue weiti, xixue weiyong* ('Chinese learning for substance, Western learning for use'). This view—known as the *tiyong* concept—displays ambivalence, suspicion and even some contempt for foreign knowledge and skills. The concept persists in Chinese thinking today and suggests that foreign ideas are beneficial only in their practical or technical applications but have no transcendent qualities that are relevant to China. Deeply rooted values thus continue to place constraints on China's military modernization through foreign acquisitions.

Presenting further complications is the present-day environment in which China must seek to resolve these old dilemmas. On the one hand, China's own strategists recognize that the country enjoys the most favourable security environment it has known for over 150 years. This benign international environment has also contributed to the country's dramatic economic growth and to related social and economic reforms. On the other hand, the pace of change in military technology and doctrinal requirements has accelerated tremendously, as have their costs in terms of financial, material and intellectual challenges. In spite of positive economic, social and security-related developments, China appears ill-prepared to meet these new challenges.

Nevertheless, the Chinese leadership is determined to reassert in the coming decades China's historical position as the region's most influential power and, looking further ahead, to re-establish its claims to great-power status. One path to achieving such influence and status which China clearly intends to take is the development of its military power, including the import of weapons and military technologies. While this is a path that China has often taken before, it is one that has equally often proven to be difficult and problematic.

What has China acquired?

By far the largest proportion of China's foreign weapons and military technologies, both quantitatively and qualitatively, has come from the Soviet Union and then Russia. This is the case in spite of the long hiatus in friendly military ties, which affected arms transfers, between Moscow and Beijing from 1960 until the late 1980s. China has also received weapons or military technology from a number of other sources, including such Western countries as France, Germany, Italy, the United Kingdom and the United States, as well as Israel and countries in the developing world such as Egypt, Iran and Pakistan. However, with the possible exception of recent transfers from Israel to China, these Western and developing world sources of weapons have proved to be problematic and their supplies relatively limited in terms of quantity and quality. Thus, in its continuing effort to maintain a credible and relatively modern fighting force, China has had to rely almost entirely on weapons and technology based on 1950s and 1960s designs imported from the Soviet Union. From this relatively weak technological base, it will be difficult for China to make significant strides forward in military modernization without further foreign sources of weapons and military technology.

Events in recent years have contributed to an environment that is more conducive to the import of weapons and technologies from the Soviet Union and, later, Russia as well as from such sources as Israel. These events include: the isolation of China by the Western allies in the wake of the Tiananmen Square tragedy of June 1989; the collapse of the Soviet Union and the cold war order; the normalization of Sino-Soviet/Russian relations; and the continuing improvement of China's economy and international political status throughout the first half of the 1990s. However, while certain Chinese purchases of foreign weapons gained considerable attention from the international community, there remained numerous questions as to the long-term extent and nature of these acquisitions, and how and whether China could translate them into significant military gains for the future. Moreover, reliance on these recent events to explain current developments may fail to take into account the continuing influence of China's historical experience with arms imports.

China's capabilities and intentions

While China has proved its capabilities to develop relatively advanced systems—such as ballistic missile, rocket and nuclear weapon technology—analysts both inside and outside of China point to the relatively poor quality of the Chinese military arsenal taken as a whole. This situation was caused by a number of factors, including the doctrinal requirements of the People's Liberation Army (PLA) up until the mid-1980s, China's heavy reliance on the Soviet Union during its period of defence industrial development, and its long history of difficulties in effectively translating foreign weapons and weapon technology procurement into an indigenous capacity to produce advanced weapons and technology.

Until the mid-1980s, China's arms purchases reflected its long-held conventional military doctrine, which prepared for 'People's War'—a primarily defensive doctrine envisaging conflict with adversaries invading mostly over land. Under such a doctrine, the vastly superior numbers of very inferior weapons which were produced by Chinese defence factories might have served as a suitable conventional deterrent. However, as the doctrine changed and came to embrace new concepts about the nature and likelihood of future warfare, so too came the need for China to modernize militarily, in part through the import of weapons and military technologies. As described in this report, these new concepts required improved naval and air capabilities; improved command, control, communication and intelligence; better air and sea surveillance; in-flight refuelling capabilities; and rapid airlift and mobility. The perceived need for these and other military capabilities meant that China would have to look abroad for assistance either with off-the-shelf arms imports or with technology transfers.

As a result, China's military capabilities are gradually being strengthened, and the import of weapons and weapon technologies is an important factor in this development. However, this point should be balanced by another: that China is faced with the dilemma of reconciling its strategic intentions with its arms import and production capabilities. China continues to bear a more than 150-year-old burden in finding an acceptable balance between indigenous weapon development, on the one hand, and importing 'superb and secret weapons', on the other.

III. Structure of the report

In addressing the three principal questions set out at the beginning of the chapter, this study contributes to narrowing a gap in the understanding of security-related issues regarding China. First, very little is known about China's arms imports, even though, more than any other military-related factor, they may enable China to have a much more powerful influence in regional and global affairs. If analysts are to judge with greater precision what capabilities China will possess in the future, the quantity and quality of foreign weapons and weapon technology acquired by China must be given careful consideration.

Second, as China is a growing power within the international system, its rise will need to be addressed in a manner which is conducive to maintaining stability, particularly in the East Asian region. Thus, at a fundamental level, the degree to which Chinese arms imports may contribute to the country's power is a subject well worth examining as part of the overall effort to accommodate China's growing influence in the international system.

Third, this study also sheds light on more specific aspects of security related to China at the domestic, regional and global levels of analysis. At the domestic level, an analysis of Chinese arms and military technology imports will indicate how China will address the dilemmas of its defence industry, while also pointing to the political influence and strategic priorities of the Chinese military. At the regional level, Chinese arms imports take on a new significance in the light of the fast-moving yet uncharted nature of the post-cold war East

Asian security environment. In particular, China's new defence strategy to prepare for limited local wars calls for the formation of a modern force with enhanced mobility and fire-power in preparation for small-scale, low-intensity warfare in and around China's border areas. At the global level, China's arms and technology imports could have a long-term effect on international efforts to promote worldwide arms control regimes and to curb the proliferation of military technologies.

The present study relies on the most extensive open-source data and file collections available on the subject of Chinese arms and technology imports. In addition to these sources at SIPRI and other open-source information, it also relies on numerous interviews and discussions with Chinese and Western experts both in China and elsewhere. A study of this nature delves into sensitive subjects. Information and data are often difficult to come by, a situation which is particularly true with regard to China. As a result, while the transactions listed in appendix 1 are those for which there is strong confirmation, the study makes a limited number of references to deals for which some of the details may be uncertain. Data on arms or technology transfers from countries such as Iran and Pakistan are not only scarce but very difficult to confirm. Even though information on Chinese arms acquisitions is incomplete, this study provides the most comprehensive and in-depth single volume on the subject.

Following this introductory chapter, the remainder of the study is divided into four chapters. Chapters 2–4 are both documentary and analytical in nature and present data on and explanations of China's foreign arms acquisitions over time. Chapter 2 provides an historical summary of Chinese foreign arms acquisitions from the late Qing Dynasty period (the middle of the 19th century) to the establishment of the People's Republic of China (PRC) in 1949. It also assesses Chinese arms imports in the framework of Sino-Soviet cooperation in the 1950s. The chapter ends with a discussion of China's efforts to acquire weapons and weapon technology from the West during the 1970s and 1980s.

Chapters 3 and 4 take up developments from 1989 to the mid-1990s. Chapter 3 documents and assesses the warming military relationship between China and the Soviet Union/Russia during this period, particularly its effect on the transfer of Soviet and Russian weapons and military technology to China. In addition, an assessment

of the causes and long-term implications of closer military cooperation between Moscow and Beijing is offered. Chapter 4 addresses
contemporary Chinese arms imports from sources in the West and the
developing world in this period. Contrary to widely held opinion,
China has continued to receive weapons and military-related technologies from the West. The extent of such transfers from other
sources requires closer scrutiny.

Chapter 5 examines the future of Chinese foreign arms acquisitions
from four broad perspectives. Considered first are the important
domestic influences which are likely to affect future Chinese arms
acquisitions, including economic, technological, administrative and
political influences. Second, important international determinants are
examined, including sources of supply, external developments and
Chinese threat perceptions. Third, the chapter suggests the foreign
arms acquisition decisions that are likely to be made in the light of
domestic and international influences and, fourth, it addresses the
implications of Chinese foreign arms acquisitions for regional
security in the years ahead.

The last section of chapter 5 presents several broad conclusions.
First, efforts to understand the determinants and directions of Chinese
arms acquisitions from abroad need to consider China's historical
experience, which provides both incentives for and limitations on
foreign procurement. Second, for both historical and contemporary
reasons, China will continue to have considerable difficulties in
translating its foreign weapon procurement into a modern military
force or modern arms industry. China's arms imports can supplement,
but will not supplant, its long-term goal of self-reliance in defence
modernization. Finally, this report concludes that China's quest for
advanced foreign weapons and weapon technology is part and parcel
of its long-held regional and global ambitions and thus will continue
to be a significant aspect of Chinese security planning.

2. Lessons of history: 150 years of foreign arms acquisitions

In the face of these difficulties, should we continue our scientific research, especially the high-tech defence projects . . .? . . . Some people said that the difficulties were so many and so formidable that we should slow down the development of sophisticated defence techniques. . . . My attitude was clear throughout: For more than a century, imperialists had bullied, humiliated and oppressed China. To put an end to this situation, we had to develop sophisticated weapons . . . (Nie Rongzhen, Marshal of the PLA, 1985[1])

I. Introduction

It is useful to study contemporary Chinese arms and technology imports within the larger historical context of China's lengthy effort to strengthen its military capabilities through cooperation with foreign partners. The profound historical and cultural influence of China's past affects contemporary developments in important and persistent ways. Many of the questions and debates of the past which revolved around the relationship between military modernization and foreign assistance remain prominent problems today. In an examination of Chinese arms acquisitions, three important factors guide the search for insights from China's historical experience.

1. If technological progress is understood to be a relatively linear process which often relies on the step-by-step advance of knowledge and skills based on the application of previously gained knowledge, then China's history since the mid-19th century has not been conducive to the smooth or rapid development of such a process. China has still not recovered from more than a century of calamity, disruption, conflict, ideological struggle and plunder, which have restrained its technological progress. This experience and its effects raise fundamental questions as to whether China can ever 'make up for lost time'.

2. Chinese policy makers themselves remain acutely aware of the influence of history on contemporary events. Perhaps the most power-

[1] From Nie Rongzhen, *Inside the Red Star: The Memoirs of Marshal Nie Rongzhen* (New World Press: Beijing, 1988), p. 702.

ful of their memories is the spectre of the 'century of shame', judged by China's current regime to have lasted roughly from the period of the Opium Wars and the first achievement of spheres of influence in China by foreign powers in the middle of the 19th century until the triumph of Mao Zedong and the Chinese Communist Party (CCP) in 1949. The bitter recollection of China's humiliating relationship with foreign powers during this period powerfully influences not only China's attempts to re-establish itself as a great and respected power but also its struggle to achieve this goal as much as possible by its own efforts. China's sour experience with Soviet military-related assistance in the 1950s and with similar assistance from the West in the 1970s and 1980s did little to dispel the lingering Chinese memories of ill-treatment by foreigners. Such historically derived attitudes have important implications for current arms import policies in China.

3. The historical isolation of China from much of the rest of the world throughout most of its long history has led to a measure of suspicion and distrust in China of foreign ideas and influence. Such feelings were strengthened by the view that China was at the 'centre of the world' in all respects, and it was not given to accepting the supposed superiority of things foreign. Such deeply rooted tenets also had a bearing on how acquisitions of foreign weapons and weapon technology would proceed.

The rest of this chapter briefly reviews China's historical experiences, beginning with the century prior to 1949, continuing with the more contemporary periods of Sino-Soviet cooperation in the 1950s, and concluding with Sino-Western cooperation in the 1970s and 1980s.

II. Arms imports before 1949

The Qing Dynasty turns to the West

The development of a modern arms industry in China which incorporated foreign designs and techniques can be dated from the mid-19th century. This military modernization was rooted in the 'self-strengthening movement' led by the Confucian scholar and reformer Feng Guifen and was implemented largely by Qing officials such as Lin Zexu, Li Hongzhang, Zeng Guofan and Zuo Zongtang. Feng's reform measures were broad in scope but specifically included military modernization, particularly in ordnance production, through the use of certain foreign capital equipment and manufacturing techniques.[2]

As early as the 1840s, in the wake of the disastrous first Opium War, the prominent military reformer and Imperial High Commissioner Lin Zexu recognized the need for China to modernize its means of defence through the purchase and adaptation of foreign weapons and weapon production techniques. He was responsible as early as 1840 for the purchase of 'more than 200 foreign guns [cannon] from every country in the West' (but probably of English and Portuguese origin) for the unsuccessful defence of Canton in 1841.[3] Lin was also responsible for China's purchase of an English merchant ship which was then used as a model for the development of Chinese-built warships. He hired staff to translate foreign documents on weapons and technologies, and he energetically lobbied his government to provide the necessary resources to build up China's defence through arms imports. In 1844, he proposed:

Let us now, in this time of peace, adopt the superior skill of the barbarians in order to control them with greater effect . . . One or two foreign 'eyes' from France and America should be invited to bring foreign artisans to Canton to supervise the construction of ships and to manufacture firearms. . . . western pilots should also be invited to train men in navigation and gunnery. Then there should be a careful selection of clever artisans and good sailors from Fukien and Kwangtung to learn these things: the artisans for construction and manufacturing work, and the sailors to learn sailing and naval operation.[4]

---

[2] On this point and in support of the following discussion, see Wang Li *et al.* (eds), *Dangdai Zhongguo de Bingqi Gongye* [Contemporary China's ordnance industry] (Dangdai Zhongguo Chubanshe: Beijing, 1993), pp. 1–9; Frey, H., *L'armée Chinoise* [The Chinese Army] (Librairie Hachette et Cie: Paris, 1904), pp. 47–74; Chen, G., *Lin Tse-Hsü: Pioneer Promoter of the Adoption of Western Means of Maritime Defense in China* (Yenching University: Peiping, 1934); Michael, F., *Li Hung-chang and the Huai Army* (University of Washington Press: Seattle, Wash., 1964); Kennedy, T. L., *The Arms of Kiangnan: Modernization in the Chinese Ordnance Industry, 1860–1895* (Westview Press: Boulder, Colo., 1978); and Frankenstein, J., 'The People's Republic of China: arms production, industrial strategy and problems of history', ed. H. Wulf, SIPRI, *Arms Industry Limited* (Oxford University Press: Oxford, 1993), especially pp. 271–75. See also Frankenstein, J., 'Back to the future: a historical perspective on Chinese military modernization', Paper presented to the annual meeting of the International Studies Association, Anaheim, Calif., Mar. 1986.

[3] Chen (note 2), p. 11.

[4] Quoted in Chen (note 2), pp. 5–6.

Wei Yuan, Lin's contemporary, put it succinctly: 'Develop skills to defeat the foreigners' (*zhangji yi zhiyi*).[5] These early efforts and ideas were to have a profound effect on subsequent military modernizers such as Li Hongzhang and Zeng Guofan.

In the spring of 1864, the commander of the Huai army and Governor of Jiangsu, Li Hongzhang, observing the strategic threat posed to China by foreign weapons and weapon technology, wrote to his prince: 'I consider that if China wishes to make herself strong, then there is nothing more important than study and practice with the excellent weapons of the foreign nations. To learn about these foreign weapons, there is no better way than to seek the machines which make machines and learn their way [of making them] but not employ their personnel'.[6]

Of critical importance to the strategies of such modernizers was the insistence that China not simply import complete weapon systems but also learn from foreign production techniques in order to establish a self-sufficiency in arms production—an across-the-board capability which required modernization not only in producing the weapons themselves but throughout the entire production cycle, from prospecting and mining raw materials, to transportation and communications infrastructures, to efficient manufacture, and to maintenance, logistics and support of weapons in the field. In the last half of the 19th century, with the aid of foreign expertise and technology from Great Britain, France, the United States and other countries, China made great strides towards achievement of the self-strengthening goals.

In particular, in this period arsenals were created in Shanghai, Tianjin and throughout Jiangsu province which by 1875 were producing weapons ranging from rifles based on Remington and Mauser designs, to coastal defence guns of large calibres, to iron-clad steamships and water mines. In the early years of the 20th century, a French military officer in China noted that the arsenals at Hanyang and Jiangnan were running with the assistance of European engineers and technicians. The Hanyang arsenal could manufacture 50 Mauser rifles and 25 000 ammunition cartridges a day and had an annual production of about 100 cannon. At this time, under the guidance of several British advisers, the Jiangnan arsenal produced rifles and

[5] Wang *et al.* (note 2), p. 8.
[6] Quoted in Kennedy (note 2), p. 41.

ammunition and had an annual output of about 20 heavy cannon based on English naval designs, as well as 100 rapid-fire Grüson-model cannon of small calibres.[7]

However, in spite of such achievements, these industries were plagued by problems of poor indigenous management skills and lack of centralized leadership; a shortage of trained Chinese manpower; the high costs of foreign materials, fuel and expertise; and the low quality and even dangerous nature of the products. In addition to these problems, official Chinese accounts blame the corrupt practices of Qing Dynasty officialdom and 'bureaucratic feudalism' as root causes of China's failure to make significant technological progress in its arms production capacity.[8] Ultimately, in spite of significant gains in production capabilities, these larger problems contributed to China's inability to withstand further military humiliation at the hands of foreign powers at the end of the 19th and beginning of the 20th centuries. While the production-specific problems could be addressed through foreign techniques, the more profound needs of modernization and reform at a macroeconomic and societal level had to be carried out by the Chinese themselves. The dependence on foreign expertise and technology was a source of China's fears as well as a source of its modernization. As Thomas Kennedy concludes, writing about Chinese military modernization in the latter half of the 19th century: 'Imperialism made rapid modernization of the ordnance industry a survival issue for China, but rapid modernization could take place only under the tutelage of the imperialist powers and through reliance on their men, machinery, and material'.[9]

This dilemma is best understood in relation to the *tiyong* concept raised in chapter 1. This concept illustrates the tension which comes from seeking to balance that which is in essence Chinese against that which is needed from foreign sources. This tension exists across all facets of China's relationship with the West. With arms production and military modernization, the *tiyong* concept at the same time both drives and restrains China's efforts to improve its capabilities through foreign inputs by seeking to maintain a significant measure of Chinese self-reliance and 'substance', while gaining what is useful from foreign sources. The concept reflects an ambivalence towards

---

[7] Frey (note 2), pp. 47–49.
[8] Wang *et al.* (note 2), pp. 7–8.
[9] Kennedy (note 2), p. 160.

foreign learning and suggests that certain foreign ideas are usel their practical or technical applications but are not appropriate fo. ... deeper conceptual roots of Chinese thinking and study. From the mid-19th century to the present day, the concept has exerted a powerful influence on China's approach to military modernization through the acquisition of weapons and weapon technologies from abroad.

Warlords and civil war

The interval between the fall of China's last dynasty in 1911 and the ascent to power of the Communists in 1949 was marked by intense periods of civil unrest and warlordism, the Japanese occupation of Manchuria (1931–45), Japan's subsequent invasion of and all-out war with China (1937–45) and the Chinese Civil War (1927–49). These events largely contributed to a significant flux of foreign weapons to China and prevented the Chinese from developing an effective and productive military production capability.

Three broad points may serve to clarify the developments related to Chinese arms acquisitions from abroad in this period. First, during the final years of the Qing Dynasty Chinese weapon and military technology manufacturers were unable to translate foreign assistance into an effective indigenous weapon-making capability because of such constraints as poor management, a lack of centralized leadership, manpower shortages, lack of capital and the high costs of foreign inputs. The collapse of dynastic rule and the onset of political and social chaos which followed only exacerbated an already disastrous situation. While some arsenals had made significant advances in technology and production, the results at the national level were mixed and uneven, and the productive arsenals still could not come close to meeting national needs in either quantity or quality.

An official Chinese account gives an indication of the difficulties the country faced:

The Qing government appointed Liu Zuocheng and Li Baojun, both of whom returned from Japan, to set up a factory in Nanyuan, [a] southern suburb of Beijing, to manufacture aircraft in 1910. The first aircraft was witnessed in April of the following year, but . . . crashed during a flight test due to engine failure. This was the very beginning of modern aircraft manufacture in China.[10]

According to Chan, in 1916 'there were twenty-nine arsenals [in China], only eight of which actually possessed the machinery to produce armaments and ammunition. The remainder were capable of simple repair work and storage'.[11] Thus the baseline for arms production at the end of the Qing Dynasty was relatively low.

Second, continual devastation wrought by internal and external forces further hindered China's development of an indigenous arms production capability. The impact of Japan's conflict with China had a disastrous effect on China's ability to develop its military production capability. Throughout most of the first half of this century Japan maintained a strong influence over the economic development of Manchuria, an area rich in industrial potential. With the outright occupation of Manchuria by Japan in 1931, the potential contribution of this region to the development of an indigenous arms production capability was lost to China until the end of the Pacific War in 1945. China's most highly developed and productive arsenal of the warlord period, the plant based in Shenyang, came into Japanese hands when Japan seized Manchuria.

Moreover, the invasion of China by Japan in 1937 led to the massive destruction of major parts of China's industrial base. The major industrial cities of eastern China were devastated by bombing and artillery attacks in the late 1930s. What was left of China's industrial base was salvaged and carted piece by piece into China's interior, first to Hangzhou and later to Chongqing. With the end of the Pacific War, the long-simmering Chinese Civil War was resumed with renewed intensity, hindering the Communists and Nationalists from developing new defence industrial capacities.

From these first two points follows the third: the perpetual conflicts not only hindered foreign-assisted military modernization but also generated a continuing strong dependence on off-the-shelf foreign weapon systems to prosecute war efforts. Between 1911 and 1949 numerous international sources of supply—both private and official—poured finished weapon systems into China, first to warlord govern-

---

[10] Duan Zijun *et al.* (eds), *China Today: Aviation Industry* (China Aviation Industry Press: Beijing, 1989), p. 7.

[11] Chan, A. B., *Arming the Chinese: The Western Armaments Trade in Warlord China, 1920–1928* (University of British Columbia Press: Vancouver, 1982), p. 110.

ments and then to the Nationalist and Communist forces. These suppliers included governments and individuals from Belgium, Czechoslovakia, Germany, Italy, Japan, the UK, the USA and the USSR.

Little in the way of technology transfer or indigenous development was offered or gained in these arrangements. Those partnership arrangements which did seek to assist the indigenous development of the defence industries of either certain warlords or the Nationalists suffered heavy setbacks with the onset of the war with Japan in the mid-1930s. As the Chinese war against Japan intensified from the late 1930s, the USSR and particularly the USA provided massive amounts of finished weapons and military aid to China but comparatively little in the way of training or development of indigenous production capacities. In any event, the chaos, corruption and utter collapse of order in this period made any serious effort at reform or modernization nearly impossible.

The earlier years of this period, from around 1911 to 1927, were marked by the often violent disunity of warlordism and presented opportunities for the arms trade in China for commercial, military and political reasons: (a) with the end of World War I in 1918, arms suppliers searched for new markets; (b) not only were weapons in high demand among the military leaders in China to prosecute their internal conflicts, but the new and more deadly technologies developed and implemented in World War I appealed to warlords bent on asserting their power; and (c) the political entities which were party to the arms trade—foreign and warlord governments alike—believed that the commerce in weapons was a means of gaining influence and ascendancy in this politically chaotic period.[12]

Recognizing the instability of China in the early warlord period, several foreign governments with interests in China reached a UK-initiated arms embargo accord in May 1919. The Arms Embargo Agreement was first signed by the governments of Brazil, France, Japan, Portugal, Spain, Czarist Russia, the UK and the USA, and had the support of other governments such as those of Belgium, Denmark, Italy and the Netherlands. However, the embargo was soon violated, and the violations were often blatant and executed with the knowledge and support of signatory governments, although most of the

---

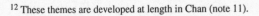

[12] These themes are developed at length in Chan (note 11).

trade was commercial rather than government-to-government in nature.[13]

In the early 1920s, warlords in China imported relatively large quantities of weapon systems and some limited means of production. These imports included hundreds of thousands of revolvers, rifles and machine-guns, millions of rounds of ammunition, hundreds of artillery pieces, dozens of aircraft, military vehicles (including tanks and trucks), spares for these systems, as well as other military equipment and stores. In spite of these large numbers, however, China was a relatively small market for the world's arms exporters, ranking only fifteenth, for example, on the list of British arms recipients over the period 1923–29.[14]

Some Chinese warlords also managed to purchase machinery and expertise from abroad during this period to develop their arms production capacity. For example, finding the arsenals under his control to be technologically lacking, the Chinese warlord in north-eastern China, Zhang Zuolin, negotiated in 1921 with the Danish firm of Nielsen and Winther for 300 sets of machinery to be used in producing ammunition and weapons. By the mid-1920s Zhang's newly equipped arsenal in Shenyang could produce hundreds of thousands of rifle cartridges each day, and up to 200 artillery pieces and 300 000 shells each year, and employed hundreds of foreigners.[15] However, even though Zhang Zuolin was the most successful warlord in developing domestic Chinese weapon production and possessed the financial means to invest further in this development, he remained heavily reliant on direct imports of off-the-shelf weapons. As a whole, by the end of the warlord period, China was unable to develop a sufficiently productive indigenous arms-manufacturing capacity.

A fledgling military aircraft industry was established in China during the warlord period with the assistance of foreign hardware and expertise, but this development was not translated into a self-sufficient indigenous production capacity. Several of the early Chinese aviation pioneers were foreign-trained and returned to China to apply their knowledge to the development of China's aircraft manufacturing base. In addition, British, French, Italian, Soviet and US expertise was employed. However, most Chinese aircraft production

[13] Chan (note 11), pp. 59–65.
[14] Chan (note 11), p. 50.
[15] Chan (note 11), p. 111.

was copy-production and relied considerably on foreign investment, material, technology and expertise. Both because of and in spite of significant foreign inputs—off-the-shelf purchases and the import of certain key components, material and technological know-how—in the period 1911–49, China was unable to establish a self-sufficient aircraft industry.[16]

Following the end of the Pacific War in 1945, the two sides of the Chinese Civil War relied heavily on weapons from foreign sources— either captured or delivered—to prosecute their war against one another. When the civil war came to an end in late 1949, neither side could claim a victory in terms of an arms-production capacity, although they had acquired large amounts of foreign weapons. During the period 1946–50, the PLA captured, mainly from the retreating Nationalists, some 3 160 000 rifles, 320 000 machine-guns, 55 000 artillery pieces, 622 tanks, 389 armoured vehicles, 189 military aircraft and 200 small warships.[17]

One expert has noted that the victorious PLA march past Tiananmen Gate on 1 October 1949 was 'the most extensive public display of US military hardware in over a decade'.[18] Nevertheless, military leaders of the newly established PRC faced a serious dilemma. Even with substantial levels of weapons, the PLA was unable to successfully bring the civil war to a close. It lacked the military capacity to do so. This can be attributed in part to the country's heavy reliance on foreign sources of weaponry and technology and its consequent inability to develop its own military means. According to one account published in mainland China, in the years under the Guomindang (1927–49) China's arms industries did not make significant gains of their own and remained heavily reliant on foreign assistance. As a result, specialized Chinese expertise went unused and the scientific and technological level of the country faltered.[19] According to the official history of China's defence industry, by the end of 1949 '[t]here was actually no capability to develop and produce modern weapons such as aircraft, naval vessels, tanks, large calibre cannons

[16] Duan *et al.* (note 10), pp. 7–11.

[17] Garthoff, R. L., 'Sino-Soviet military relations, 1945–66', ed. R. L. Garthoff, *Sino-Soviet Military Relations* (Praeger: New York, 1966), p. 83.

[18] Frieman, W. 'Foreign technology and Chinese modernization', eds C. D. Lovejoy and B. W. Watson, *China's Military Reforms: International and Domestic Implications* (Westview Press: Boulder, Colo., 1986), p. 60.

[19] Wang *et al.* (note 2), p. 9.

and military electronics. New China's defence industry started on this very weak basis'.[20]

Moreover, and of greater importance for the longer term, without a well-developed military industry, China found itself increasingly vulnerable to outside threats. As was the case more than a century earlier, foreign weapons were both a threat to China's weakness and its only hope for renewed strength.

III. Soviet military assistance to China in the 1950s

Background developments

China's current weapon inventory is largely based on Soviet designs and technologies which are several decades old. However, since 1949 China has demonstrated its technological prowess in developing and deploying certain advanced systems such as ballistic missiles, nuclear-powered ballistic missile submarines and satellites. This seeming unevenness in weapon-system development stems in part from the international and domestic turbulence discussed in the previous section as well as from the massive levels of Soviet assistance provided to the Chinese defence industry in the early years of the PRC. China's experience with Soviet assistance, however, had both its good and bad points.

In 1949, ravaged by 100 years of foreign intervention and civil wars, the PRC's industrial and economic infrastructure required a massive overhaul with vast capital investment and foreign assistance. Primarily because of the growing bipolarization of world politics, China had little option but to turn to the USSR, the most developed socialist state and patron of the Communist bloc. Thus China patterned itself on the Soviet model of socialist development in restructuring the state, society and the military.

The daunting task of rebuilding China began immediately after the official proclamation of the People's Republic of China on 1 October 1949. After an unusually long stay in Moscow—two months—Mao Zedong was able to secure economic and political support from Stalin, as stipulated in the 30-year Sino-Soviet Treaty of Friendship,

---

[20] Xie Guang *et al.* (eds), *China Today: Defence Science and Technology* (National Defence Industry Press: Beijing, 1993), p. 10.

Alliance and Mutual Assistance of 14 February 1950.[21] Among other points, this treaty provided China with a five-year loan of $300 million at 1 per cent interest and the construction of 50 key projects over the next nine years, including the mining of certain metals and the extraction of oil in Xinjiang, the construction and repair of naval vessels in Dalian, and the operation of civil airlines.

In the light of China's great need for economic and technological assistance, however, the amount of Soviet aid was only a drop in the ocean. Indeed, Poland received more Soviet aid—$450 million, at no interest—than China. In addition, Stalin was 'clearly in no hurry to provide [military aid] to the Chinese in substantial quantities until compelled to do so by circumstances'.[22] The 'circumstances' turned out to be the Chinese intervention in the Korean War.

Information on Soviet military aid to China during the Korean War remains fragmentary, sketchy and contradictory, and needs to be further corroborated with the Soviet war archives which are open to the public.[23] Available sources indicate that the exigencies of war compelled the USSR to supply a substantial amount of heavy equipment, mostly artillery and tanks, and a large number of aircraft to North Korea and China. Armed with the PLA's old, but huge inventory of light weapons and artillery, the Chinese People's Volunteers (CPV) entered the war in October 1950 without Soviet military assistance. The initial casualties at the end of 1950 and particularly the heavy battle losses in early 1951 prompted PLA Chief of Staff Xu Xiangqian's visit to Moscow in May 1951 and eventually led to the October 1951 agreement for the USSR to provide massive amounts of equipment to supply dozens of Chinese infantry and airborne divi-

---

[21] For the text of the Sino-Soviet treaty, see *China and the Soviet Union, 1949–84*, Keesing's International Studies (Longman: Burnt Mill, Harlow, 1985), pp. 1–2.

[22] Joffe, E., *The Chinese Army After Mao* (Harvard University Press: Cambridge, Mass., 1987), p. 4.

[23] The recent opening of the Soviet archives on the Korean War is of particular importance. In June 1994, for instance, Russian President Boris Yeltsin hand-delivered the declassified Soviet Korean War documents to visiting South Korean President Kim Young Sam as a goodwill gesture. The documents have revealed that Chinese leaders had been more deeply involved in war planning than scholars and officials have assumed for the past 40 years: Mao agreed as early as May 1949 to transfer 3 Korean PLA divisions to North Korea and help the latter's liberation war after Chinese unification. See 'Classified Korean War documents released by the Russian Government', *Chosun Ilbo* [Chosun daily] (Seoul), seven parts, 26 July–4 Aug. 1994. An English translation is available from the authors of this research report.

sions.[24] In addition to direct transfers of weapons, this agreement also provided for Soviet expert assistance, know-how and technology to be passed to China to advance its arms-production capabilities.[25]

The total air strength of the People's Liberation Army Air Force (PLAAF) was more than tripled in size during 1951, from 500 aircraft in 1950 to more than 1500 aircraft, including some 700 MiG-15 fighter jets and about 150 Tu-2 piston-engine light bombers.[26] During the Korean War, the USSR supplied China with military aid amounting at the time to $1.5–2 billion, including aid to war industries in Manchuria.[27] As a result of the Chinese involvement in the war, China became more dependent on the USSR financially and diplomatically, and Chinese leaders sought to follow the Soviet lines of socialist development more closely than before.

The death of Stalin on 5 March 1953 and the end of the Korean War on 27 July of the same year proved to be turning-points in Sino-Soviet relations. The year also marked the beginning of China's First Five-Year Plan (1953–57). A more generous Soviet aid programme with an additional 91 projects in China was initiated in the weeks following

[24] For a Chinese account of the battlefield need for heavy equipment and aircraft, see Hong Xuezhi, *Kangmei Yuanchao Zhanzheng Huiyi* [Recollection of the war to resist US aggression and aid Korea] (Jiefangjun Wenyi Chubanshe: Beijing, 1990), especially chapter 10. Hong Xuezhi was a CPV deputy commander in charge of logistics, including armament. See also Goncharov, S. N., Lewis, J. W. and Xue, L., *Uncertain Partners: Stalin, Mao, and the Korean War* (Stanford University Press: Stanford, Calif., 1993), pp. 200–201, 346–47.

[25] Wang *et al.* (note 2), pp. 35–37.

[26] The 'bean counts' of Chinese air strength are only rough estimates because of combat losses and the Soviet assistance to the Chinese aviation industry not directly related to the Korean War. Most of the aircraft gained by China during the Korean War can be regarded as direct Soviet supply. For various estimates of the Chinese Air Force during the Korean War, see Gittings, J., *The Role of the Chinese Army* (Oxford University Press: Oxford, for the Royal Institute of International Affairs: London, 1967), pp. 121–31, 136–41; Griffith, S. B., Jr, *The Chinese People's Liberation Army* (McGraw-Hill: New York, 1967), pp. 166–71; and Garthoff (note 17), p. 85.

[27] China recently reported that during the Korean War it spent 6.2 billion yuan (about $2 billion) in direct war expense and over 10 billion yuan (about $3.3 billion) in total expenditures, direct and indirect, related to the war. China claimed that the Chinese debt for the Soviet weaponry was 3 billion yuan ($1.1 billion). These costs are presumably based on 1950s prices. The Chinese claim roughly corresponds to Western estimates. See Yang Fu, 'Number of Chinese troops and casualties in the Korean War', *Kuang Chiao Ching* (Hong Kong), 16 Apr. 1993, pp. 48–52, in Foreign Broadcast Information Service, *Daily Report–China* (hereafter FBIS-CHI), 6 May 1993, pp. 21–25, especially p. 25; Eckstein, A., *Communist China's Economic Growth and Foreign Trade: Implications for U.S. Policy* (McGraw-Hill: New York, 1966), pp. 154–55; and Gittings, J., *Survey of the Sino-Soviet Dispute: A Commentary and Extracts from the Recent Polemics 1963–1967* (Oxford University Press: Oxford, 1968), pp. 128–34.

the death of Stalin.[28] During the high-level visit to Beijing in October 1954, First Secretary Nikita Khrushchev, Deputy Premier and Defence Minister Nikolay Bulganin, and Deputy Premier and Trade Minister Anastas Mikoyan further expanded the scope of the Soviet aid programme to China, including the signing of the scientific–technical agreement and assistance on 15 new industrial projects. Mikoyan's April 1956 visit to China resulted in a Soviet commitment to an additional 55 projects. An agreement signed in August 1958 porovided for the construction or expansion of an additional 47 metallurgical, chemical and machine-building industries (MBIs)—bringing the total number of Soviet projects in China to 258 by 1958.[29] Finally, the February 1959 agreement envisaged Soviet assistance on 78 additional undertakings, 31 more than in the previous agreement, for the period 1959–67; apparently none of the 31 new projects was completed when Soviet technicians withdrew from China in August 1960. Soviet military aid to China in the 1950s probably amounted to between one-quarter and one-half of the total aid to China during this period.

A notable increase in the nature and extent of the Soviet aid to China after the death of Stalin strongly indicates that Stalin's successors were far more inclined to supply China with better weapons and technological know-how than Stalin, who had kept China militarily and financially dependent on the USSR by providing mostly finished products and spare parts. From 1953 to 1956 the Soviet aid programme included the wholesale transfer of blueprints, prototypes, expertise and personnel for China's burgeoning defence industries.

Soviet assistance in China's weapon-producing capability was referred to by one Western analyst as 'the largest technology transfer experiment in history'.[30] Others noted that the Soviets 'gave their Chinese allies the best they had available'.[31] While China and the USSR offered differing accounts, the Soviet aid programme to China in the 1950s no doubt included a massive transfer of equipment, technological know-how and personnel. According to Soviet

[28] Dittmer, L., *Sino-Soviet Normalization and Its International Implications, 1945–1990* (University of Washington Press: Seattle, Wash., 1992), p. 18.

[29] The number of Soviet projects reported to have been under way in China differs from one source to another. Agreements for a total of 258 projects were formally signed between China and the Soviet Union by the end of 1958.

[30] Frieman (note 18), p. 55.

[31] Griffith (note 26), p. 178.

accounts, the USSR helped China develop more than 250 key industrial projects: between 1954 and 1963 the USSR provided China with over 24 000 sets of scientific and technological documents and assisted work at 1400 large industrial enterprises, and more than 10 000 Soviet specialists in various scientific fields visited China between 1950 and 1960.[32] The same source claimed that between 1951 and 1962 some 10 000 Chinese engineers, technicians and skilled workers, and over 11 000 students, were educated and trained in various Soviet institutions of higher learning, research centres and industrial enterprises, as well as some additional 8000 Chinese for short-term training. Other sources estimate the total number of Chinese students and trainees who studied in the USSR in the 1950s to be as high as 38 000.[33]

With this assistance, in the 1950s China began to build up its own indigenous weapon-production capability. From the outset, the Chinese defence industry closely followed the Soviet organizational model and followed the classic development path of weapon production—from simple assembly, to spare-parts production, to co-production under licence, and eventually to the production of complete weapon systems. However, the growth of China's defence industry showed some distinctive features in terms of organization, leadership control and resource allocation.[34] For example, the majority

[32] The official Soviet account was given on 14 Feb. 1964 during a speech to the Central Committee of the Communist Party of the Soviet Union (CPSU) by Mikhail Suslov, a chief ideologue on the Sino-Soviet dispute. See Suslov, M., 'The struggle of the Communist Party of the Soviet Union for the unity of the international communist movement', *Pravda*, 3 Apr. 1964. Excerpts of the speech are available in Gittings (note 27), pp. 134–35. Suslov's speech was rejected by China, which claimed that the leaders of the CPSU 'unscrupulously withdrew the 1,390 Soviet experts working in China, tore up 343 contracts . . . scrapped 257 projects of scientific and technical co-operation, all within the short span of a month'. See 'The reply of the Central Committee of the Communist Party of China to the CPSU letter', 29 Feb. 1964, *Renmin Ribao*, 9 May 1964; excerpts are reproduced in Gittings (note 27), pp. 55, 139–40.

[33] Quested, R. K. I., *Sino-Russian Relations: A Short History* (George Allen & Unwin: Sydney, 1984), pp. 124–25; and Dittmer (note 28), pp. 21–22.

[34] For an historical overview of China's defence industry, see Ostrov, B. C., *Conquering Resources: The Growth and Decline of the PLA's Science and Technology Commission for National Defense* (M. E. Sharpe: Armonk, N.Y., 1991); Frieman, W., 'China's military R&D system: reform and reorientation', eds D. F. Simon and M. Goldman, *Science and Technology in Post-Mao China* (Harvard University Press: Cambridge, Mass., 1989), pp. 251–86; Latham, R. J., 'People's Republic of China: the restructuring of defense–industrial policies', ed. J. E. Katz, *Arms Production in Developing Countries: An Analysis of Decision Making* (D. C. Heath and Company: Lexington, Mass., 1984), pp. 103–22; and Shambaugh, D., 'China's defense industries: indigenous and foreign procurement', ed. P. H. B. Godwin, *The Chinese Defense Establishment: Continuity and Change in the 1980s* (Westview Press: Boulder, Colo. 1983), pp. 44–47, 54–69.

of the defence plants were located in China's interior (the so-called Third Front) to protect them from possible US attack and to promote balanced development among different regions.[35] In addition, the rapid expansion of defence production by the mid-1950s gave rise to problems of leadership control over and policy coordination in the defence industry. The leadership's response to these problems resulted in a series of organizational changes in China's defence industry.

In October 1958 the National Defence Science and Technology Commission (NDSTC) was created with Nie Rongzhen as its chairman. The NDSTC mainly focused on research and development (R&D) of new and advanced weapons, especially nuclear weapons. In 1960, the National Defence Industry Office (NDIO) was established to coordinate the production of conventional weapons at various defence factories under six MBIs. As Benjamin Ostrov's study of the NDSTC demonstrates, the organizational/theoretical separation between R&D and weapon production was one thing, but the reality was quite another.[36] Not only did the holistic and continuous nature of weapon R&D and production make the organizational division of labour untenable, but the NDSTC had overlapping and competing jurisdiction over China's defence industry with the NDIO. While the launching of the Great Leap Forward (1958–60) and the withdrawal of Soviet advisers in 1960 elevated the importance of the NDSTC in China's defence industry, the initial organizational division was to significantly contribute to the uneven development of China's weapon systems in the coming decades.

Development of the PLA with Soviet assistance

Development of the PLA Navy

China's naval and air force development illustrates how PLA military capabilities were given a massive boost by Soviet assistance in the 1950s. When the Chinese Communists declared victory in 1949, there was no national PLA Navy (PLAN).[37] The nascent naval force con-

---

[35] On the 'Third Front' see Naughton, B., 'The Third Front: defence industrialization in the Chinese interior', *China Quarterly*, no. 115 (Sep. 1988), pp. 351–86.

[36] Ostrov (note 34), pp. 30–33.

[37] The historical account of the PLA Navy is drawn from the PLA Navy History Editorial Committee, *Haijun Shi* [History of the [PLA] Navy] (PLA Publishers: Beijing, Sep. 1989),

sisted of 4000 former Nationalist Navy personnel who were captured or defected in 1948–49, and fewer than 100 out of the 200 ships were operable. Training centres were set up on a regional basis. Following the formation in November 1948 of the first naval force, the North-East Navy, another regional navy, called the East China People's Navy, was created on 23 April 1949, with veteran Army General Zhang Aiping as its commander and political commissar. The national PLAN headquarters in Beijing was not established until 14 April 1950, with Xiao Jingguang as its first commander.

The early Soviet assistance programme included the creation of the Soviet Naval Advisory Mission in Beijing and the dispatch of 500 naval advisers and maintenance personnel in 1950. In July 1950, the Soviet Union began to deliver naval weapons, equipment and spare parts for the nascent PLAN. The first Soviet transfers of finished naval craft consisted of about 50 World War II-vintage torpedo boats, which took place in 1951. The PLAN's first submarine was the non-operational Soviet M Class, shipped to China in July 1953. According to one source, China received an additional eight S-1 and M-V Class submarines in 1954–55.[38]

From 1955, Soviet naval assistance to China picked up pace, with Chinese assembly of Soviet Whiskey Class submarines and Riga Class frigates from components provided by Soviet shipyards. At the time of the Soviet withdrawal in August 1960, the PLAN's inventory comprised 350 surface ships and submarines. It included about 12 submarines directly transferred from the USSR and 19 Whiskey Class submarines assembled in Chinese shipyards, 4 Soviet Gordy Class destroyers, 4 Riga Class frigates (assembled in Chinese shipyards), 20 Kronstadt Class large patrol craft (14 assembled in Chinese shipyards), some 150 patrol craft (most assembled in China) and about 30 minesweepers (some 26 assembled in China).[39]

In the mid-1950s, with Soviet assistance, China made some gains in establishing an indigenous shipbuilding industry. One prominent example of this effort was the founding on 1 July 1956 of the

pp. 14–27. See also Yang Guoyu et al. (eds), Dangdai Zhongguo Haijun [Contemporary China's naval forces] (Zhongguo Shehui Kexue Chubanshe: Beijing, 1987), pp. 3–153.

[38] Muller, D. G., Jr, China as a Maritime Power (Westview Press: Boulder, Colo., 1983), pp. 29–30. Gardiner, R. et al. (eds), Conway's All the World's Fighting Ships, 1947–1982, Part 2 (Conway Maritime Press: London, 1983), p. 333 notes that China received 6 M Class, 4 SHCH Class, and 4 S Class submarines from the Soviet Union in 1954–55.

[39] See Muller (note 38), p. 40; Haijun shi (note 37), pp. 336–37; and appendix 1 in this volume.

Shanghai Institute of Shipbuilding. This organization subsequently produced the first Chinese-designed naval craft in 1959, the Shanghai Class coastal patrol boat. By the end of the 1950s, China was able to develop a modest operational naval force to such a point that a US intelligence assessment asserted: 'The years since 1949 have brought a fantastic growth in Chinese Communist naval power, so much so that for the first time in modern history China is a factor in the Far Eastern naval picture'.[40] While these developments in PLA naval capability might be considered 'indigenous', Soviet assistance was decisively important.

Development of the PLA Air Force

The growth of Chinese air power in the 1950s also illustrates the extensive nature of Soviet aid.[41] In the period 1946–49, the number of Communist Chinese military aircraft fluctuated widely owing to war losses, captures and defections by Guomindang pilots. By the end of the war there were fewer than 200 aircraft left. According to official Chinese accounts, the new regime in Beijing in late 1949 could lay claim to approximately 159 foreign aircraft—US, British, and Japanese—including P-47 and P-51 fighters, Japanese 'Oscar' fighters, B-24 and B-25 bombers, as well as transports and trainer aircraft, although many of these aircraft were not operational.[42] In addition, the PLA was able to capture from the retreating Guomindang some 1278 aircraft engines and more than 40 000 tonnes of aviation equipment and supplies, nearly all of which was of foreign origin.[43]

The establishment of the PLAAF was formally announced on 11 November 1949, with Liu Yalou as its first commander and Xiao

---

[40] US Office of Naval Intelligence (ONI), *ONI Review*, Secret Supplement, spring–summer 1957, p. 44, as cited in Muller (note 38), p. 32.

[41] For a historical and organizational review of the PLA Air Force, see US Defense Intelligence Agency, *People's Republic of China People's Liberation Army Air Force*, report no. DIC-1300-445-91 (DIA: Washington, DC, May 1991); PLA Air Force Headquarters Editorial and Research Office, *Kongjun shi* [History of the [PLA] Air Force] (PLA Publishers: Beijing, Nov. 1989); Wang Dinglie, *et al.* (eds), *Dangdai Zhongguo Kongjun* [Contemporary China's Air Force] (Zhongguo Shehui Kexue Chubanshe: Beijing, 1989); and Bueschel, R. M., *Communist Chinese Air Power* (Praeger Publishers: New York, 1968). Bueschel's is a pioneering study of the PLA Air Force. His 238-page book, however, does not reveal any sources for its information; its account needs to be corroborated with other sources. On the development of the Chinese aviation industry, see Duan *et al.* (note 10).

[42] Wang *et al.* (note 41), table 2, p. 38.

[43] Duan *et al.* (note 10), p. 15.

Hua as its political commissar. Premier Zhou Enlai assessed the aircraft production situation and issued instructions:

Construction of China's aviation industry should be carried out according to the Chinese practical situation . . . We could not just rely on buying foreign aircraft and only carrying out repair by ourselves. The construction road, therefore, of China's aviation industry should be conducting repair first, manufacture afterwards and then the design . . . certain consideration should be given to the planning and arrangement of turning [repair facilities] into a manufacture factory in the future. Meanwhile, negotiations should be carried out with the Soviets about their assistance for the construction of our aviation industry.[44]

Thus, from the outset the PLAAF was closely reliant on the USSR for equipment and manufacturing techniques. The PLAAF also became reliant on the Soviet Union for organization, doctrines and training.

As was the case with Chinese military modernization in general, the Korean War was a catalyst in the rapid development of Chinese air power in the 1950s. PLAAF strength grew rapidly: in February 1953 US intelligence estimates placed Chinese air strength at 1400 combat aircraft, including 830 jet and 250 piston engine fighters, excluding the combat losses of well over 1000 fighters.[45] According to US Air Force data, the Far East Air Force Command 'destroyed 976 and damaged 1009 enemy [Chinese and North Korean] aircraft in air-to-air combat' during the entire Korean War.[46] Even after the war, Soviet supply of aircraft to China continued unabated. Including the introduction of the MiG-17 in late 1954, the PLAAF inventory reached about 4000 aircraft by late 1955, of which over 2000 were fighters and the remainder bombers, transports and support aircraft of varying types.

The effort to produce a combat aircraft in China began with the establishment of the Second MBI's National Aircraft Factory in Shenyang in 1951. In the early 1950s assembly lines with Soviet components were set up for Yak-18 primary trainers, which began to appear in 1954. Based on agreements signed during Khrushchev's October 1954 visit to China, the USSR supplied China with produc-

---

[44] Quoted in Duan *et al*. (note 10), p. 16.
[45] See Bueschel (note 41), pp. 26–27.
[46] As cited in US Defense Intelligence Agency (note 41), p. F-42. On the other hand, the PLA Air Force 'shot down 330 aircraft and damaged another 95' during the Korean War. See *Kongjun shi* (note 41), pp. 84–85.

tion licences, engineering drawings and technical aid for the production of Chinese aircraft. Accordingly, the Chinese aircraft-production
capability grew rapidly to include the production of engines under
licence and complete aircraft. By the autumn of 1956, China had produced its first combat aircraft, the J-4 (based on the Soviet MiG-17).[47]
Between 1956 and 1960, China had licence-produced some 2000 of
these aircraft.[48]

J-4

China also began to take delivery of the more advanced Soviet
MiG-19 fighters in 1959. Production plans for the MiG-19s were
based on the October 1957 agreement between the two countries, but
this time the goal was to make the MiG-19 a 'Chinese' aircraft with
airframes, engines and armaments locally built under licence. The
Soviet withdrawal in 1960, however, brought MiG-19 production to a
complete halt. The Chinese managed to produce the first J-6 (based
on Soviet MiG-19) in December 1961—strongly suggesting that the
production lines were near completion before the Soviet withdrawal.[49]
The number of J-6 fighters in the PLAAF inventory reached 100 by
the summer of 1964 and rose rapidly thereafter.

J-6

The story of the MiG-21 is more difficult to assess. Perhaps only 20
Soviet-built MiG-21s made their way to China before the Soviet
withdrawal in August 1960, but apparently there were no production
arrangements. By the early 1960s, the PLAAF faced the problem of
creeping obsolescence. However, with no engineering drawings, spare
parts or production know-how, China exerted an enormous indigenous effort to produce its version of the MiG-21 aircraft, the J-7. By
the summer of 1967, over 100 J-7s had entered service.[50]

J-7

The first Soviet Il-28 light bomber entered the PLAAF inventory in
October 1952 and the Tu-16 medium bomber in May 1959. China
modified the designs and technical specifications of both bombers: the
Il-28 was produced in Harbin as the H-5, which entered service with

---

[47] The 'J' designation, stands for the word *jianjiji* (fighter aircraft). Similarly, the
designation 'H' (for *hongjiji*) is used for bomber aircraft. The Chinese designations are used
throughout this study, with reference to Soviet models where appropriate. The Chinese apply
Western designations (such as 'F' or 'B') when aircraft are produced for export.

[48] See appendix 1 in this volume.

[49] *Jane's Encyclopedia of Aviation*, vol. 4 (Grolier Educational Corporation: Danburry,
Conn., 1980), pp. 812–13.

[50] US Defense Intelligence Agency (note 41), p. C-5. Bueschel notes, however, that 12–15
MiG-21s entered evaluation service as early as Mar. 1965. See Bueschel (note 41), p. 89.

the PLAAF in August 1967; the Tu-16, produced in Xian as the H-6, entered service in February 1969.[51]

Nuclear weapon development

The issue of Soviet assistance to China's nuclear weapon programme has probably been the most controversial one in Sino-Soviet relations and has left an indelible imprint on the subsequent development of China's nuclear weapons, military strategy and national attitude to security. In the early years of the PRC Government, China had to rely on Soviet nuclear protection from a possible US nuclear threat. The fragility of such a commitment soon became clear to Chinese leaders as the USA increasingly threatened to use nuclear weapons. In July 1950, for instance, President Harry S Truman sent 10 nuclear-configured B-29s to US bases in the Western Pacific and in late 1950 warned China that he would take 'whatever steps are necessary' to stop Chinese intervention and that the use of nuclear weapons 'had been [under] active consideration'.[52] Truman even added, to the consternation of many, that military commanders in the field would be 'in charge of' the use of atomic weapons. China's motivation to acquire nuclear weapons was reinforced by its failure to invade Taiwan in the 1950s, foiled in part by the US nuclear threat. Taken together with the muted Soviet response during US hostility, these events must have convinced the Chinese leadership of the indispensability of nuclear weapons as a deterrent and guarantor of China's sovereignty, notwithstanding its public rhetoric that nuclear weapons were only 'paper tigers'.[53]

The Chinese decision to develop nuclear weapons came in the winter of 1954/55 and the implementation of the decision began in earnest in 1955.[54] The Ministry of Nuclear Industry was founded in

---

[51] Norris, R. S., Burrows, A. S. and Fieldhouse, R. W., *Nuclear Weapons Databook: British, French, and Chinese Nuclear Weapons, Vol. V* (Westview Press: Boulder, Colo., 1994), pp. 331–36, 366–67.

[52] Dingman, R., 'Atomic diplomacy during the Korean War', *International Security*, vol. 13, no. 3 (winter 1988/89), pp. 60–69. The quotations are on pp. 65–66.

[53] On the impact of US threats on the Chinese decision to possess nuclear weapons see Lewis, J. W. and Xue Litai, *China Builds the Bomb* (Stanford University Press: Stanford, Calif., 1988), chapter 2; and Xie Guang *et al.* (eds), *Dangdai Zhongguo de Guofang Keji Shiye* [Modern China's science and technological undertakings in national defence], vol. 1 (Dangdai Zhongguo Chubanshe: Beijing, 1992), pp. 25–26.

[54] Lewis and Xue (note 53), pp. 34–35. It is believed that in a Jan. 1955 Politburo meeting, Mao Zedong approved the development of a nuclear weapons programme after a presentation

1955,[55] and the USSR agreed in April to assist China in developing research on atomic energy and nuclear physics, the first of six nuclear agreements that China and the USSR concluded between 1955 and 1958. Beginning in March 1956, hundreds of Chinese nuclear scientists were trained at the Dubna Nuclear Research Institute in Moscow, while nuclear weapon research at the Institute of Physics and Atomic Energy in Beijing was given priority in terms of funding and personnel.[56] At the same time, the USSR continued to help China to construct a gaseous diffusion plant in Lanzhou that produced weapon-grade uranium. In September 1957, Nie Rongzhen, Chen Geng and Song Renqiong travelled to Moscow and negotiated for more than a month in an effort to obtain Soviet assistance in the development of Chinese nuclear weapons and missiles. On 15 October, during Mao's visit to Moscow, the USSR agreed in signing the New Defence Technology Pact to provide China with a sample of an atomic bomb and technical data concerning its manufacture.[57] Also agreed in the pact was the delivery of two R-2 missiles and related technical information.

By late 1957, however, the gulf between China and the USSR had widened, and in 1958–59 a rapid succession of problems plagued Sino-Soviet relations. The Soviet delivery of two R-2 missiles (SS-2s) and their blueprints in January 1958 was followed by a proposal to set up a joint military command in the Far East, which was immediately rejected by China.[58] In May 1959 the USSR delivered two Tu-16 bomber aircraft, one of which was to be assembled in China. However, on 20 June of the same year the Central Committee of the Soviet Communist Party formally notified the Central Committee of the Chinese Communist Party that the USSR would not provide China

by Qian Sanqiang, the 'father of China's atom bomb'. For a meeting summary, see Lieberthal, K. G. and Dickson, B. J., *A Research Guide to Central Party and Government Meetings in China* (M. E. Sharpe: New York, 1989), p. 24.

[55] The Ministry of Nuclear Industry was then called the 'Second MBI', one of the 6 MBIs in charge of atomic energy and weapon development. With the creation of the Third MBI in Nov. 1956, some of the Second MBI's responsibility was transferred to the Third MBI. See Lewis and Xue (note 53), p. 49. Norris *et al.* (note 51), however, note that the name of the Third MBI was changed to the 'Second MBI' on 11 Feb. 1958 (p. 331). For an overview of the organizational setups, see Zhonghua Renmin Gongheguo Hegongyebu [PRC Ministry of Nuclear Industry], 'Woguo he gongyede chuangjian yu fazhan' [The creation and development of our country's nuclear industry], ed. Renmin Chubanshe, *Guanghuide chengjiu* [Brilliant achievements] (Renmin Chubanshe: Beijing, 1984), pp. 283–85.

[56] Lewis and Xue (note 53), p. 42.

[57] Gittings (note 27), p. 106.

[58] See Norris *et al.* (note 51), p. 331; and Lewis and Xue (note 53), p. 212.

with the technical details of atomic bombs. Immediately after June 1959, China decided to develop atomic bombs with its own resources, and China's first atomic test was given the code name '596' (for the year and month of the Soviet final notice) to inspire Chinese nuclear personnel.[59]

After the USSR withdrew its experts from China in August 1960, the NDSTC took on greater responsibilities to coordinate nuclear weapon production. At the same time, the Chinese leaders devoted enormous capital and human resources to develop atomic bombs in an 'all-at-once approach': the efforts to master nuclear weapon theory, design and construction were conducted simultaneously with the development of delivery vehicles, such as ballistic missiles, aircraft and submarines. In such a crash programme, one failure in any stage or area would have had a ripple effect on the entire endeavour. Notwithstanding such risks, China finally exploded its first experimental atomic bomb at Lop Nor on 16 October 1964. China's first hydrogen (thermonuclear) bomb was successfully tested on 17 June 1967.[60]

The end of the 'honeymoon': lessons of overdependence

The Sino-Soviet relationship, while never perfect, dramatically changed for the worse from 1958. An open rift developed with the withdrawal of Soviet advisers, aid and blueprints in 1960, and there were Sino-Soviet border clashes in the late 1960s. The bitterness of the dispute—framed in terms of ideological disagreements, divergent national interests and conflicting domestic political imperatives—was to taint the relationship for decades. Indeed, the dispute would have a profound influence on Chinese policies regarding arms imports in a way which strengthened historical lessons about such foreign assistance.

---

[59] Norris, *et al.* (note 51), p. 337. The Soviet rebuff in June 1959 and subsequent deterioration in Sino-Soviet relations in the early 1960s provided inspiration to the Chinese bomb-making effort. In crediting the Soviet attitude in the development of China's nuclear weapons, Mao Zedong is said to have joked that China should award Khrushchev 'a massive, one-ton medal'. Nie (note 1), p. 701.

[60] See the Chinese nuclear chronology in Norris *et al.* (note 51), pp. 331–36. See also Lewis, J. W. and Hua Di, 'China's ballistic missile programs: technologies, strategies, goals', *International Security*, vol. 17, no. 2 (fall 1992), pp. 5–40.

Analysts of the Sino-Soviet rift differ on the importance of ideology in determining the split.[61] However, the 1969 border clashes seemed to confirm the clear divergence of national interests between China and the USSR which began over the issues of the 'inevitability of war', Soviet assistance in China's nuclear development and the 1958 Taiwan Strait crisis. Armed conflict between the two giants fed the dispute over national interests which would last for nearly 30 years. Moreover, in the late 1950s China and the USSR adopted different paths of socialist development, with the attendant efforts to export their respective 'models' to the Third World. At the personal power level, Mao's political position became increasingly vulnerable after the dismal failure of the Great Leap Forward (1958–60), while Khrushchev's power fluctuated even more widely than Mao's between the 1956 intervention in Hungary and the 1962 Cuban Missile Crisis. Greatly affected by these political crises, Sino-Soviet relations went from bad to worse.

Whatever the root causes, the abrupt Soviet withdrawal was a severe blow to the defence modernization of China. In August 1960, all 1390 Soviet experts were withdrawn from China, which left 257 scientific and technological cooperation projects incomplete and 343 technical aid contracts cancelled.[62] High-pitched exhortations to self-reliance, a recurrent theme in the modern history of Chinese defence industrial development, resurfaced on a national scale and were then the only recourse. Accordingly, in the early 1960s the Chinese defence industry underwent a major reorganization with the formation of eight functionally specific machine-building industry ministries: the First and the Eighth MBIs in charge of civilian production; the Second MBI, nuclear energy and weapons; the Third MBI, aircraft; the Fourth MBI, electronics and radar; the Fifth MBI, ordnance and artillery; the Sixth MBI, naval vessels; and the Seventh MBI, ballistic missiles.[63] The organization of the MBIs reflects the Chinese leader-

---

[61] Donald Zagoria, e.g., argues that ideology was a major factor in both facilitating and sustaining the conflict. Others, such as William Griffith, treat ideology as a dependent variable, deriving from what they see as more important national security factors. Lowell Dittmer, citing the armed clashes in 1969, depreciates the ideological dimension of the Sino-Soviet conflict. See, e.g., Zagoria, D. S., *The Sino-Soviet Conflict, 1956–1961* (Princeton University Press: Princeton, N.J., 1962); and Griffith, W., *The Sino-Soviet Rift* (MIT Press: Cambridge, Mass., 1964).

[62] See 'The letter of the CCP CC to CPSU CC', in Gittings (note 27), pp. 139–40.

[63] Specific production responsibilities of each MBI varied slightly because of a series of major reorganizations between the late 1950s and the early 1960s. See Shambaugh (note 34), pp. 44–47, 54–69; Jammes, S., 'Military industry', eds G. Segal and W. T. Tow, *Chinese*

ship's commitment to a long-term investment in strategic as well as major conventional hardware.

Like the Soviet aid programme itself, the abrupt withdrawal of that aid had an enduring impact on China's arms import policy for the coming decades. Deprived of this source of modern foreign technology, China had to resort to its own scientific and technical means to provide the requisite weapons and equipment to the PLA. Even if China had gained invaluable experience in mass-producing conventional weapons in the late 1950s, its inability to produce indigenous weapon systems became all too clear after the Soviet withdrawal in 1960. As Nie Rongzhen noted looking back to Sino-Soviet defence production cooperation in the 1950s:

[T]he Soviet Union wanted to keep its lead over us and had misgivings about us. So it was imposing ever tighter restrictions on us concerning sophisticated technology for national defence. . . . They only permitted us to copy weapons they had stopped or would soon stop producing, and would not provide us with any new equipment they were producing or developing. Their assistance to our research and development was limited to letting us copy a few prototypes. In short, they wanted to keep us forever in the status of an imitator and an appendage, always two or three steps behind them. . . . In view of these changes in Sino-Soviet relations, I considered how we should develop our science and technology independently.[64]

Given the lack of indigenous production capability and foreign sources for weapons, the only plausible solution was to gradually modify and improve the existing weapon inventory through reverse-engineering. This involves the painstaking process of taking a foreign weapon system entirely apart, developing blueprints for each part and then attempting to reproduce the system based on indigenous designs and production processes. Reverse-engineering is a gargantuan task, requiring huge investments of capital and manpower, and is an especially time-consuming process. Moreover, the long process of reverse-engineering hindered innovation, new design skills and the absorption of more modern technology, as it mostly involved copying procedures, revealing little in the way of 'know-how' or 'know-why'. By definition, reverse-engineering could not improve on the technologies that had not been incorporated in the finished weapon system

Defense Policy (University of Illinois Press: Urbana, Ill., 1984), pp. 124–28; and Frankenstein, in Wulf (note 2), pp. 279–80, 282–83.

[64] Nie (note 1), pp. 698–99.

under reconstruction. In fact, most modern high-technology weapons are not as susceptible to labour-intensive reverse-engineering as the 1950s-vintage weapon systems have been. China's continuing lack of progress in electronics, communications and radar technology was in part caused by its heavy reliance on the reverse-engineering method pursued since the early 1960s. Under such difficult circumstances, the leadership's best choice was to devote limited human and capital resources to a few major projects. Examples in this category include ballistic missiles, nuclear submarines and commercial satellites, which can be termed the 'pockets of excellence'. In all other categories of conventional weapons and equipment, China had to face the growing problem of obsolescence.

Moreover, the combined effect of the abrupt Soviet withdrawal and the dismal failure of the Great Leap Forward was keenly felt throughout the MBIs in the early 1960s. According to a study by Chu-Yuan Cheng,[65] the MBIs' estimated gross output value declined by 60 per cent from 1960 to 1961. While the MBIs began to recover in 1964, their output value in 1966 was still about 10 per cent below the level of 1960. Applying a different indicator, the MBIs' annual average growth in 1957–66 in terms of gross output value was 12.3 per cent, which was less than half that of the First Five-Year Plan (1953–57), 31.1 per cent.[66]

By the mid-1960s, with China's defence industry returning to some normalcy, the Cultural Revolution (1966–76) set in. Despite the wishes of the central leadership to shield military industry from the undiscriminating attacks of the Red Guards, the Cultural Revolution seriously disrupted military production. In addition, not only did its long duration keep an entire generation of scientists, technicians and engineers from schools and laboratories, but its anti-foreign nature also prohibited the Chinese defence industry from taking advantage of advanced technology available at the international level, particularly during the height of social upheaval between 1966 and 1969.[67]

---

[65] Chu-Yuan Cheng, 'Growth and structural changes in the Chinese Machine-Building Industry, 1952–1966', *China Quarterly*, no. 41 (Jan.–Mar. 1970), pp. 46–48.

[66] Cheng (note 65), p. 48.

[67] Lewis and Xue, among others, discuss the damage brought by the Cultural Revolution to the development of China's nuclear weapon programme. See Lewis and Xue (note 53), pp. 214, 236. See also Ostrov (note 34), pp. 36–37, 91; Shambaugh (note 34), p. 47; and Su Wenming (ed.), *China's Army: Ready for Modernization* (Beijing Review: Beijing, 1985), p. 19.

Finally, the difficult lessons of China's overdependence on the USSR in the 1950s left an indelible imprint on the minds of Chinese leaders and inculcated in them a painful awareness of the political and security dangers of overdependence on a single supplier of weapons and weapon technology. The acquisition of Soviet weapons and technology was out of the question for nearly three decades to come, while China's caution towards other foreign weapon suppliers was further strengthened.

IV. New foreign sources, 1975–89

Background developments

Beginning in the mid-1970s and continuing until the late 1980s, China was active in seeking weapons and weapon technologies from the developed world. However, while the Chinese did a good deal of 'window shopping' during this period, very little was actually purchased. The difference between interest and actual purchases reveals much about the potential and limits for Chinese arms acquisitions from abroad.

Owing to the 'years of neglect' during the Cultural Revolution, post-Mao Chinese leaders inherited over four million troops with questionable morale and combat readiness, a poor defence production capability, a demoralized R&D community, a huge inventory of obsolete weaponry and the anachronistic Maoist People's War strategy. These defects and more were very evident during the débâcle of China's punitive war against Viet Nam in 1979. Clearly there was a need for military modernization both within the armed forces and in the production sector, and the acquisition of foreign weapons and technologies was seen in China as one way of contributing to the process. Fortuitously, the international strategic environment of the 1970s favoured a warmer relationship between China and the West, including the transfer of military hardware and technology to the PRC.

As another factor, changes in PLA strategic doctrine required the purchase of more modern equipment. China's military leadership realized that the People's War strategy—based on the assumption of 'an early war, a large-scale war, and a nuclear war'—was not suited to the limited warfare which China was likely to face and that the PLA needed to become a smaller, better-trained, better-equipped and more mobile force with enhanced manœuvrability and fire power designed to meet the requirements of 'local conflicts' (*jubu zhanzheng*) of varying degrees of intensity and duration. Formally enunciated at the June 1985 meeting of the CCP Central Military Commission (CMC), this policy had gathered strength since the mid-1970s.[68]

Limited transfers from the West

In spite of these needs, a number of domestic and international factors combined to limit Chinese arms acquisitions from the West during the period from the mid-1970s to the late 1980s.

One factor was China's resistance against overdependence on foreign-based help, deriving not only from the sour experiences of Sino-Soviet relations but also from the other important cultural, ideological, bureaucratic and national security considerations raised at the beginning of this chapter. However, this did not preclude the import of foreign weapons and weapon technologies; as Wendy Frieman and others noted at the time, the Chinese military modernization policy of the mid-1980s pragmatically recognized the need for a 'two-track' policy which sought to acquire foreign technologies to address specific needs over the short term, while making a commitment to developing and advancing indigenous R&D and production capacities over the long term.[69]

In this regard, Defence Minister Zhang Aiping's March 1983 declaration in *Hongqi*—exhorting China to become self-reliant in modernized defence production but acknowledging the need to learn from some foreign technologies—is a key statement of Chinese thinking at the time.[70] William Tow summarized the problem well when he wrote

---

[68] For the text of Deng Xiaoping's speech at the enlarged meeting of the CMC, see *Deng Xiaoping Wenxuan* [Selected works of Deng Xiaoping], vol. 3 (Renmin Chubanshe: Beijing, Oct. 1993), pp. 126–29. China's current security strategy is based upon the decisions made in this landmark meeting, which included the reassessment of the international situation, the continuation of troop reductions and the reorganization of military regions. The meeting also reaffirmed that national economic development had priority over defence modernization. While Deng Xiaoping acknowledged the necessity of military equipment modernization, he cautioned: 'We need to be patient for [the next] few years'; *Deng Xiaoping Wenxuan*, p. 128.

[69] Frieman (note 18), p. 65.

[70] See 'Defence minister calls on China to develop its own weapons', in British Broadcasting Corporation, *Summary of World Broadcasts*, FE/7272/BII/I, 6 Mar. 1983; and 'Zhang Aiping writes on defense modernization', in FBIS-CHI, 7 Mar. 1983, pp. K3–K4, originally published in *Hongqi* [Red flag], 1 Mar. 1983, p. 1.

China's ability to apply modern technology to its strategic requirements 'will be largely determined by how adept that country's pragmatists will be in neutralizing domestic resistance to interacting with those external sources best able to provide China with potential instruments of power'.[71]

A second factor to consider relates to the lack of 'absorptive capacity' in China. On the whole the Chinese remained technically deficient in their ability to absorb, manage and integrate advanced armaments from abroad, a problem that was not new.[72] In particular, the impact of the Cultural Revolution on the development of skilled expertise only served to exacerbate problems of absorptive capacity: not only did the chaos of the period interrupt the stream of trained experts and technicians coming into the defence production workforce, but many experts already engaged in defence production were prevented from conducting research and testing. By the late 1970s and early 1980s, the efforts of Chinese defence industries to close the technological gap between Chinese and Western and Soviet military R&D and production through the absorption of foreign weapons and technology were slowed.

Third, China lacked the economic means to import large amounts of weapons and technology. With military modernization last on the 'Four Modernizations' priority list—coming behind improvements in agriculture, industry, and science and technology—the Chinese defence budget declined or remained stagnant during the period 1977–89 and declined as a percentage of total government spending from 1981 to 1989 by 50 per cent.[73] Faced with such budget restrictions, China found it difficult to allocate the necessary funding to modernize the armed forces through foreign acquisitions.

Fourth, the shift in Chinese strategic perceptions at the turn of the 1980s which foresaw the likelihood of limited conventional war meant a focus on fewer, more capable weapons, and not on large-scale purchases. Finally, supply-side restrictions—such as those related to the Co-ordinating Committee on Multilateral Export Con-

[71] Tow, W. T., 'Science and technology in China's defense', *Problems of Communism*, July–Aug. 1985, p. 31.

[72] See, e.g., Simon, D. F., 'China's absorption of foreign technology: prospects and problems', eds N. Ginsberg and B. A. Lalor, *China: The 80s Era* (Westview Press: Boulder, Colo., 1984); and Heymann, H., *China's Approach to Technology Acquisition: Part III—Summary Observations* (Rand Corporation: Santa Monica, Calif., Feb. 1975), pp. 37–38.

[73] US Arms Control and Disarmament Agency, *World Military Expenditure and Arms Transfers, 1991–1992* (US Government Printing Office: Washington, DC, Mar. 1994), p. 58.

Table 2.1. Arms imports by China, Taiwan, Japan and India, 1975–89
Figures are in current US$ m., and as a share of total imports (TI) for the years indicated.

Year	China Value	% of TI	Taiwan Value	% of TI	Japan Value	% of TI	India Value	% of TI
1975	110	1.6	160	2.7	60	0.1	180	2.8
1976	160	2.9	160	2.1	180	0.3	490	8.6
1977	100	1.5	180	2.1	120	0.2	725	10.9
1978	90	0.9	200	1.8	170	0.2	280	3.6
1979	180	1.2	200	1.4	230	0.2	490	5.0
1980	170	0.9	625	3.2	340	0.2	825	5.6
1981	130	0.6	550	2.6	650	0.5	1 100	7.1
1982	70	0.4	700	3.7	600	0.5	2 800	18.9
1983	100	0.5	480	2.4	775	0.6	1 300	9.2
1984	490	1.9	400	1.8	950	0.7	1 300	9.1
1985	650	1.5	575	2.9	1 000	0.8	2 600	16.3
1986	575	1.3	390	1.6	825	0.6	3 200	20.8
1987	625	1.4	1 300	3.7	1 000	0.7	3 000	18.0
1988	300	0.5	1 100	2.2	825	0.4	3 700	19.3
1989	250	0.4	525	1.0	1 700	0.8	3 900	19.0
Total/ average share	4 000	1.2	7 545	2.3	9 425	0.5	25 890	11.6

Sources: US Arms Control and Disarmament Agency (ACDA), *World Military Expenditures and Arms Transfers, 1991–1992* (US Government Printing Office: Washington, DC, Mar. 1994), table II; ACDA, *World Military Expenditures and Arms Transfers, 1989* (US Government Printing Office: Washington, DC, Oct. 1990), table II; and ACDA, *World Military Expenditures and Arms Transfers, 1986* (US Government Printing Office: Washington, DC, Apr. 1987), table II.

trols (COCOM) and national arms export regulations and prohibitions prevented or constrained the West from providing China with certain advanced weapons and weapon technologies.

These obstacles are reflected in the relatively modest level of China's arms imports during the period 1975–89 when compared with those of neighbouring countries (see table 2.1), and as indicated by the data drawn from appendix 1 and shown in table 2.2. Notably, most of the arms transfers shown in table 2.2 were quantitatively small transfers, were 'one-off' transfers of little lasting importance, and involved systems of little offensive value. Thus, while China showed

Table 2.2. Chinese imports of major conventional weapons, weapon components and weapon technology, by supplier and weapon type, 1975–89

Source/Year(s) of delivery	Number/Weapon type imported or licence-produced				
	Aircraft	Land systems	Naval systems	Radar/electronics	Missiles/Other
Canada					
1986	3 Challenger trspts				
1988–89	2 Challenger trspts				
Egypt					
1977		1 BMP-1 AIFV			3 SAM systems
					6 portable SAMs
					6 AT-3 ATMs
1978	2 MiG-23 fighters	2 T-62 MBTs			
	4 MiG-21 fighters				
	2 Su-20 fighters				
France					
1977–78	16 SA-321-H Super Frelon hels				
1982	1 AS-365N Dauphin hel				
1982–89	45 AS-365N Dauphin hels (*LP*)				
1985–86	6 AS-332 Super Puma hels				
1985–89	3 SA-321H Super Frelon hels (*LP*)				
1986				5 Rasit E radars	
1986–88 (?)		AIFV turret upgrade			
1987–89	A-5K avionics upgrade				
1988–89	8 SA-342L Gazelle hels				96 HOT-2 ATMs

Country / Period				
Germany				
1976–77	4 Bo-105C hels			
1984–89	V-8 diesel engines (LP)			
Israel				
1983–89	Avionics, AEW and in-flight refuelling assistance	MBT gun and fire-control upgrades	ELINT and EW assistance (?)	Missile technology assistance (?)
Italy				
1985 (?)			40 A-244S launchers and torpedoes	
1986–89	A-5M avionics upgrade			
United Kingdom				
1975	2 Spey 202 jet engines			
1979–89	200+ F-7M avionics upgrade			
1984				Sea Skimmer target drones
1984–86		AIFV turret upgrade	Ship-board radio systems	
1985		T-59 MBT turret upgrade		
1987		4 105-mm main guns for MBT	1 Watchman radar	
United States				
1979	9 Bell 212 hels			
1982	3 Citation II trspts			
1984–85	24 S-70C hels			

Source/Year(s) of delivery	Number/Weapon type imported or licence-produced				
	Aircraft	Land systems	Naval systems	Radar/electronics	Missiles/Other
1985	6 Bell 206B hels				
1985–89		Technical advice in munition production	Technical assistance on torpedoes		
1986–87			LM2500 gas turbines		
1986–88		AIFV turret upgrade			
1986–89	A-5M avionics upgrade				
1987	5 Learjet reconnaissance/trspts				
1987–89	J-8II avionics upgrade				
1988	2 L-100-30 Hercules trspts			2 AN/TPQ-37 artillery-locating radars	
1988–89	Initial assistance on Super-7 fighter				

Abbreviations and acronyms: AEW = airborne early warning; AIFV = armoured infantry fighting vehicle; ATM = anti-tank missile; ELINT = electronic intelligence; EW = electronic warfare; hel(s) = helicopter(s); LP = licensed production; MBT = main battle tank; SAM = surface-to-air missile; ShAML = ship-to-air missile launcher; trspts = transports.

Sources: Jane's All the World's Aircraft (Jane's Information Group: Coulsdon, Surrey, several editions); *Jane's Fighting Ships* (Jane's Information Group: Coulsdon, Surrey, several editions); *Jane's Armour and Artillery* (Jane's Information Group: Coulsdon, Surrey, several editions); and the SIPRI arms trade database, 1994.

interest in Western weaponry during this period, few purchases resulted. China's efforts to build a modern army and defence industrial base continued to be a protracted process.

The high price, in the Chinese view, of Western weapons is the most often cited reason for the sluggish sales to China. Actual sales of weapons from the West contrasted sharply with the rhetoric from Western observers which in the mid-1980s envisioned transfers of anti-tank and anti-air missiles (including the possibility of licensed production of US TOW anti-tank missiles), tactical and surveillance air defence radar systems, and high-technology computers.

According to one analysis, of 25 major arms sale negotiations between the West and China in the period 1972–81, only nine resulted in deliveries.[74] By 1985, owing in part to the perception in the West and in China that the Soviet threat had diminished, and to the persisting Chinese constraints noted above, analysts foresaw that Western military sales to China were unlikely to increase.[75] At the same time, while bureaucratic and ideological resistance to arms imports appeared to have diminished in China, in the mid-1980s the Chinese had reformulated their conditions for military imports (prompt delivery, high technology and low prices) in a way that tended to restrain rather than open the possibilities for direct off-the-shelf sales.

Acquisitions from the United States

In the early 1980s, the absence of any major direct transfers of complete weapon systems from the USA to China can be attributed to cutbacks in the Chinese defence budget, the low priority of defence in the Four Modernizations programme, US red tape involved in allowing weapon sales, and China's interest in weapons and technologies other than those offered by Washington.[76] However, in the mid- to late 1980s, US–Chinese military assistance cooperation made a number of strides forward. In the most successful US–Chinese commercial arms deal, the Sikorsky Corporation delivered 24 S-70C Black-

---

[74] Middleton, D., 'China still sparing in arms purchases', *International Herald Tribune*, 17 Feb. 1981, p. 1.

[75] Mann, P., 'Study forecasts no change in weapons sales to China', *Aviation Week & Space Technology*, 15 July 1985, p. 24.

[76] See the analysis in Parks, M., 'Sales of U.S. military gear to China fail to materialize', *Los Angeles Times*, 17 Apr. 1981, p. 1; and Graham, V., 'Arms offer will not spark buying spree', *South China Morning Post*, 24 June 1981, p. 5.

hawk helicopters in a transaction worth $140 million. Other small deals were also agreed in this period, including the transfer of small numbers of transport and VIP aircraft, as well as a small number of helicopters (see appendix 1).

In addition, four US Foreign Military Sales (FMS) programmes were initiated in the late 1980s, although these programmes were never finished.[77]

1. The most prominent FMS programme was the Peace Pearl Program. This programme, initiated by the US Air Force and worth $550 million, contracted Grumman Aerospace to provide systems definition and full-scale development of 55 avionics and fire-control kits for Chinese J-8II fighter aircraft as well as provide management services, operational support and support equipment, initial spares, and flight and related computer software data. Grumman subcontracted Westinghouse to develop 55 fire-control systems, including an AN/APG-66 radar, fire-control computer, back-up control system, databus and fire-control radar. According to one Air Force spokesman at the time, the deal would include components comparable to early F-16 technology.[78] The deliveries of the kits were to take place in early 1992.

2. In a 1987 deal valued at $28.5 million, the US Department of Defense contracted Hamilton/Bulova to assist China in a large-scale ammunition modernization programme, comprising production equipment, technical support and technical data, including assistance in the development of fuses, detonators, primers, ammunition shells and explosives.

3. In a US Army-managed programme worth $62.5 million, the Hughes Aircraft Corporation was selected as the prime contractor to sell to China 4 AN/TPQ-37 artillery-locating radars, 8 AN/VRC-46 radio sets, related support equipment, spare parts and a maintenance programme. Training of Chinese military personnel for this programme was conducted at Fort Sill in Oklahoma.

4. Honeywell was contracted to provide four Mk46 Mod. 2 anti-submarine torpedoes and related testing equipment. This torpedo was

[77] See Wilborn, T. L., *Security Cooperation with China: Analysis and a Proposal* (Strategic Studies Institute, US Army War College: Carlisle Barracks, Pa., 25 Nov. 1994); and Woon, E. Y., 'Chinese arms sales and U.S.–China military relations', *Asian Survey*, June 1989.

[78] Lachica, E., 'China will buy U.S. equipment for jet fighters', *Wall Street Journal*, 6 Aug. 1987, p. 21.

at the time widely deployed in the US inventory; it was a lightweight, high-speed, deep-diving weapon capable of being fired from surface ships or aircraft and capable of multiple re-attacks if it failed to hit its target on the initial attempt.[79]

These four FMS programmes were all suspended before completion following the Tiananmen Square crackdown in June 1989. Of the four, the ammunition modernization programme was the closest to completion. The Peace Pearl Program had already run into problems before June 1989, including cost overruns and subsequent soured relations between US and Chinese counterparts.[80] None of the torpedoes had been delivered by Honeywell, but Hughes had delivered two of the four radar sets.

Three major US commercial military sales were initiated in the late 1980s, but they were also cancelled as a result of the Tiananmen crisis. Cadillac Gage Textron and the China National Machinery Equipment Import Export Corporation announced in late 1988 their intention to develop jointly a new made-for-export main battle tank (MBT) based on the Chinese T-59 and to be called the Jaguar. In the second commercial military deal, in 1988 Grumman initiated a programme aimed at assisting China in developing the Super-7 fighter (an upgraded version of the J-7). Assistance included feasibility studies and preliminary recommendations on the aircraft. Third, under an agreement reached in March 1989, six CH-47D Chinook helicopters were to be shipped to China. As with the FMS programmes described above, the Grumman Super-7 programme, the Cadillac Gage Textron Jaguar MBT programme and the transfer of Chinook helicopters were all cancelled following the Tiananmen crackdown.[81]

Acquisitions from Europe

The transfer of European weapons and technologies to China was similarly sporadic and problematic during this period. By the end of

---

[79] *Jane's Weapon Systems, 1988–89* (Jane's Information Group: Coulsdon, Surrey, 1988), p. 535.

[80] Unknown to Grumman, each of the 50 J-8 aircraft cockpits was unique, so that each retrofit needed specialized modifications to be properly integrated, which considerably increased the cost of the programme.

[81] The Jaguar MBT development programme continued without Chinese participation.

the 1970s, in spite of an extensive courting of one another, the only significant technology transfer between China and European suppliers was the agreement signed at the end of 1975 to licence-produce the Rolls-Royce Spey 202 supersonic afterburning turbofan engine in China, including the initial provision of several completed engines with spare parts. The Spey 202 was similar to the engine powering the F-4M Phantom fighter in use with the British Royal Air Force. The deal, valued at approximately £100 million ($222 million at 1975 exchange rates), was to include the construction of a new production plant. Initially, this programme envisaged large-scale licensed production of the engine and, eventually, Chinese self-sufficiency in production and operation. However, by 1980 only one engine was known to have been completed by the Chinese, and by the mid-1980s the programme had come to a halt and no serial production had begun. Yet, up until that time, the Spey engine deal remained the 'bellwether of Sino-Western military co-operation'.[82]

Another problematic technology cooperation programme involving a European supplier was an avionics upgrade deal led by an Italian manufacturer. Aeritalia (later Alenia) assisted China under a 1986 agreement with the China Aero Technology Import–Export Corporation (CATIC) to modernize the avionics of the Q-5II Fantan attack aircraft. This upgraded aircraft was intended for export and was designated the A-5M.[83] The Italian contribution was to include the provision of an all-weather navigation and attack system similar to that used in the AMX close air support aircraft co-produced by Italy and Brazil. The system was to include weapon aiming for air-to-ground attack and air-to-air combat, passive electronic countermeasures and friend-or-foe identification capability. The programme was set back considerably by the crash of the first prototype in 1988, but after further completion of co-development and flight tests, two prototype aircraft were displayed in early 1991. China claimed in 1993 to have developed an upgraded A-5M, although it is not clear to what extent this version utilizes Italian technologies from the initial programme begun in 1986.[84]

[82] Tow, W. T., 'Arms sales to China', Segal and Tow (note 63), p. 149.
[83] The 'Q' designation is for the word *qiangjiji* (attack aircraft); the export version carries the Western 'A' designation.
[84] See Lambert, M. (ed.), *Jane's All the World's Aircraft, 1994–95* (Jane's Information Group: Coulsdon, Surrey, 1994), p. 56. Myanmar began taking delivery of 24 A-5Ms in 1994.

Several European military export deals faltered in the period to 1989 as well—the Sino-British deal to arm Luda Class destroyers with Sea Dart missiles, radars and electronics, the British offer of Sea Harrier jet aircraft and the attempted sale of French Mirage 2000 fighters being three main examples.

On the other hand, some Sino-European projects fared better. Most prominent among these programmes in the period prior to 1989 are the Sino-French agreement to licence-produce the SA-365 Dauphin 2 helicopter and the Sino-British agreement to upgrade avionics on the F-7M fighter. The helicopter programme was completed in the early 1990s, and the avionics upgrade was largely completed before June 1989. Sino-French military production cooperation involved the licensed production in Harbin of military helicopters for use by PLA services; they were known in China as the Z-9A Haitun. Following an agreement reached in July 1980, the manufacture of this helicopter began in 1982, and the initial contract for 50 helicopters was filled by January 1992. The Chinese Z-8 helicopter, for which limited production began in 1989, is based on the French SA-321H Super Frelon (originally flown in the 1960s), but no official licensing agreement was concluded for this production.

The British GEC avionics upgrade of the J-7, to be known as the F-7M, met with success as CATIC and GEC collaborated for over 10 years from 1979 in providing avionics equipment for Chinese aircraft (the avionics suite includes the Type 956 head-up-display/weapon-aiming computer—HUDWAC—and Skyranger short-range air-to-air missile/gun combat control radar), in addition to training, flight testing support and the establishment of local production plants for avionics packages.[85] The total value of these transactions between 1980 and 1989 was estimated at $168 million, and it is believed that some 200 or more Chinese aircraft were upgraded as a result of this programme.[86]

Non-Western sources

The most important foreign military imports to arrive in China during the period 1975–89 were perhaps not from countries of the indus-

[85] Lambert (note 84), pp. 47–48.
[86] 'China (People's Republic)', *Milavnews*, Oct. 1989, p. 6; and 'China (People's Republic)', *Milavnews*, Apr. 1989, p. 7.

trialized West but from Egypt and Israel. China benefited from soured Soviet–Egyptian relations in the early to mid-1970s by receiving small shipments of Soviet weaponry in return for the provision of arms and spares compatible with Egypt's Soviet-supplied armaments (see table 2.2 and appendix 1). Egyptian shipments of aircraft, armour and missiles gave China the opportunity to reverse-engineer and develop its own versions, most notably in the form of improved aircraft (upgrading the J-7), armour (the WZ-501 armoured infantry fighting vehicle), anti-tank missiles (the Hong Jian 73) and portable surface-to-air missiles (perhaps the HN-5).

Extensive but secretive Sino-Israeli cooperation, perhaps beginning as early as the mid-1970s and lasting throughout the 1980s, was believed to have resulted in the improvement of several Chinese weapon systems, including the upgrading of Chinese tanks with 105-mm guns and fire-control systems, the sale of advanced missile technology and jet fighter radar technology related to the Lavi fighter programme. While this cooperation was consistently denied by Chinese and Israeli authorities, their military production relationship was embarrassingly revealed with reports that a team of Israeli military scientists had been caught by Hong Kong authorities in November 1987 travelling to Beijing on false passports to negotiate transfers of Israeli missile technology (Sino-Israeli cooperation is treated more extensively in chapter 4).[87]

Lessons learned

From the mid-1970s to 1989, China had mixed results in its efforts to modernize its military through the acquisition of foreign weapons and technologies. Such imports were rather unsystematic and handled in a piecemeal fashion, and the assimilation of Western technologies into the outdated Chinese defence industry turned out to be a Herculean task. China's low-cost, selective approach to Western arms and tech-

[87] On Sino-Israeli military cooperation prior to 1989, see, e.g., Lau, E., 'Who blew the gaff?', *Far Eastern Economic Review*, 8 Sep. 1988, p. 23; Colvin, M., 'Israel sells radar to China in secret deal', *Sunday Times* (London), 10 Apr. 1988, p. 17; 'Rabin denies report of missiles deal with China', *Times* (London), 4 Apr. 1988, p. 6; Horowitz, D. and Black, J., 'Major arms sale to U.S.; secret deal with China reported', *Jerusalem Post International Edition*, 9 Apr. 1988, p. 1; Walker, J., 'False passports expose arms deal', *South China Sunday Morning Post*, 3 Apr. 1988, p. 1; Swain, J., 'Israel in secret missile deal with China', *Sunday Times* (London), 3 Apr. 1988, p. 1; and 'Israel's links with China', *Jane's Defence Weekly*, 10 Oct. 1987, p. 832.

nology was aimed at maximally utilizing its current inventories, which were based on 1950s Soviet technologies, designs and production methods. However, most Western technologies were invariably expensive and quite different in nature. Moreover, the production of advanced weapon systems requires high-level coordination among various horizontal units, integration of R&D and manufacturing, and skilled workers. This cannot be achieved without massive importation of Western engineering and design methods.[88]

More important, by the end of the 1980s the inherent limitations of the selective acquisition of Western arms and technology became apparent to both China and the Western countries. From the Chinese leaders' point of view, not only did the Western governments restrict the transfer of high-technology weapons to China but the imported equipment often had lower efficiency than initially expected and was hard to absorb and reproduce.[89] The Western countries for their part became increasingly frustrated with China's extensive shopping excursions which resulted in few concrete deals. Western countries were also wary of the prospect that China would eventually use the imported technology to boost its arms sales to the developing countries. A sharp increase in the volume of China's arms sales during the second half of the 1980s only heightened this concern.[90]

Whatever hope could be held out for Western arms exports to China was almost completely snuffed out as a result of two critical events in the late 1980s and early 1990s: the Tiananmen Square massacre and the collapse of the Soviet threat. These events further weakened an already weak basis for Chinese imports of weapons and technologies from the West.

[88] For a discussion of the overall capability of China's defence industry, see Frieman, W., 'China's defense industries', *Pacific Review*, vol. 6, no. 1 (1993), pp. 51–62; and Humble, R. D., 'Science, technology and China's defence industrial base', *Jane's Intelligence Review*, Jan. 1992, pp. 3–11.

[89] Simon, D. F., 'China's acquisitions and assimilation of foreign technology: Beijing's search for excellence', in Joint Economic Committee, Congress of the United States, *China's Economic Dilemmas in the 1990s: The Problems of Reforms, Modernizations, and Interdependence* (M. E. Sharpe: Armonk, N.Y., 1992), pp. 565–98.

[90] As measured by SIPRI trend-indicator values in 1991, the value of China's arms exports in the period 1986–90 was more than the value of the preceding 14 years of Chinese arms transfers combined. See Gill, R. B., *Chinese Arms Transfers: Purposes, Patterns, and Prospects in the New World Order* (Praeger: Westport, Conn., 1992), p. 38.

3. Contemporary Chinese arms and technology imports from Russia

> As for the sale of weapons, Moscow does not intend to abandon this profitable international market. Russia needs hard currency, so why not get it by selling modern armaments to China. (Remarks attributed to Russian ambassador to China Igor Rogachev, 1992[1])

> We don't want to go beyond the line that separates the sale of defensive and offensive weapons . . . we would like to preclude attempts to promote creeping, uncontrolled arms trade and to transfer technologies. (Aleksandr Shokhin, Russian Deputy Prime Minister, 1992[2])

I. Introduction

The economic capability and strategic environment that have shaped China's defence modernization in general and arms imports in particular underwent a dramatic change in the mid- to late 1980s in ways that appear favourable to Chinese relations with certain suppliers, particularly Russia. It is useful to consider briefly this background before reviewing the specific nature and scope of Chinese arms imports from Russia in the post-cold war period.

At the beginning of the 1980s, China's economic future was at best uncertain and its defence budget stagnant. In 1981, some Western defence studies estimated the cost of modernizing China's weaponry to be in the range of $41–63 billion.[3] Others concluded that China's chance of becoming a major military power by the end of century was remote, even with US assistance, and added that the gap in military capability and technology between China and the Western industrialized nations was widening.[4]

---

[1] Foreign Broadcast Information Service, *Daily Report–Central Eurasia* (hereafter FBIS-SOV), 18 Dec. 1992, p. 2.

[2] FBIS-SOV, 18 Dec. 1992, p. 9.

[3] 'U.S. military sales and technology transfers to China: the policy implications', *Mershon Center Quarterly Report*, vol. 6, no. 3 (spring 1981), p. 4. This conference report also notes that '[e]very dollar [China has] spent on technology imports must be matched by three dollars in domestic infrastructural investment in order to absorb it'; see p. 5.

[4] Stuart, D. T. and Tow, W. T., 'Chinese military modernization: the Western arms connection', *China Quarterly*, June 1982, pp. 264–65.

However, throughout the 1980s China registered the world's second highest economic growth rate (i.e., 9.4 per cent) and the highest in 1992 and 1993—12.8 per cent and 13.2 per cent, respectively.[5] In 1993 the World Bank and the International Monetary Fund reassessed China's GNP on the basis of purchasing power parity (PPP), rather than the conventional dollar conversion, and ranked the Chinese economy as the world's third largest, following the USA and Japan.[6]

During the first half of the 1990s, moreover, China was the only major power that maintained annual double-digit increases in its official defence budget. From 1989 to 1994, China's defence budget more than doubled; it rose by an annual average of over 15 per cent. China's official defence budget in 1989 was 24.5 billion renminbi (Rmb), a 12.4 per cent increase from Rmb 21.8 billion in 1988. This was followed by consecutive increases of 17.9 per cent (Rmb 28.9 billion) in 1990, 12.5 per cent (Rmb 32.5 billion) in 1991, 13.8 per cent (Rmb 37 billion) in 1992, 14.8 per cent (Rmb 42.5 billion) in 1993 and 22.4 per cent (Rmb 52 billion) in 1994. The officially announced defence budget for 1995 included a rise in spending of 14.8 per cent over the revised figure for 1994.[7] Much of these spending increases was negated by inflation and the devaluation of the Chinese renminbi in 1994. However, many analysts of Chinese mili-

[5] China's average annual GDP growth in 1980–91 was 9.4%, second only to South Korea's average annual growth of 9.6% in the same period. See *Asia 1994 Yearbook* (Review Publishing Company: Hong Kong, 1994), p. 14; and World Bank,*The East Asian Miracle: Economic Growth and Public Policy* (Oxford University Press: Oxford, 1993), p. 59. China's official announcement on its 1993 GDP growth was 13.4%. See Foreign Broadcast Information Service, *Daily Report–China* (hereafter FBIS-CHI), 11 Mar. 1994, p. 22.

[6] Greenhouse, S., 'New tally of world's economies catapult China into third place', *New York Times*, 20 May 1993. For a PPP-based assessment of the Chinese economy, see *Asia–Pacific Economic Update* (US Pacific Command: Honolulu, spring 1994), p. 91.

[7] The percentage increase is calculated from China's announced official defence budget and may differ slightly from one source to another because of rounding and exchange-rate variations. In addition, announced defence budget and actual spending at the end of the year may not be the same. For instance, China's actual defence spending in 1993 was Rmb 43.25 billion, slightly more than the original budget of Rmb 42.5 billion. Similarly, official defence spending at the end of 1994 —Rmb 55.06 billion—was 5.8% more than originally allocated. For China's annual defence budget announcements since 1989, see FBIS-CHI, 3 Apr. 1989, p. 52; 29 Mar. 1990, p. 33; 29 Mar. 1991, p. 3; 10 Apr. 1992, p. 4,; 23 Mar. 1993, p. 68; 11 Mar. 1994, p. 19; *Far Eastern Economic Review*, 5 Apr. 1990, 8 Aug. 1991, 2 Apr. 1992, 26 May 1993; *South China Morning Post* (International Weekly Edition), 19–20 Mar. 1994; and Karniol, R., 'China's defence budget continues to rise', *Jane's Defence Weekly*, 18 Mar. 1995, p. 17. For China's official position on defence spending, see Mu Huimin, 'Chinese military threat theory is totally groundless', *Renmin Ribao*, 17 Apr. 1993, p. 6, in FBIS-CHI, 28 Apr. 1993, pp. 20–21. See also US Arms Control and Disarmament Agency, *World Military Expenditures and Arms Transfers, 1991–1992* (US Government Printing Office: Washington, DC, Mar. 1994), p. 58.

tary expenditure find that the official defence budget is far lower than actual spending on the military and that the actual resource base for the military may be as much as three to five times higher than official defence budget figures.[8]

On the other hand, China's strategic environment experienced some negative developments caused by the Tiananmen Square crisis of 1989 and the end of the cold war and collapse of the Soviet Union shortly thereafter in 1991. In the view of Chinese conservatives, the Tiananmen demonstrations were a signal of the potential dangers of China's open-door policy to the West. The USA's official responses towards the crackdown, including the imposition of economic and military sanctions against China, conflicted with China's new emphasis on stability. Worse still, the passing of the cold war structure had, in the US view, greatly diminished the strategic importance of China, which would otherwise have had a soothing effect on the differences between them.

As a result, China may have found more compatibility with its counterparts in the then Soviet Union. Moreover, Soviet foreign policy since the mid-1980s—its China policy in particular—can be summed up as a series of efforts to enhance Soviet security with fewer resources.[9] During the second half of the 1980s the Soviet Union took a series of steps in relation to China that were conducive to improved relations, including the near settlement of the 'Three Obstacles' and progress in confidence-building measures and talks on

---

[8] One of the most thorough Western examinations of Chinese military expenditure to date is the China section contributed by David Shambaugh to 'World military expenditure' in Bergstrand, B.-G. *et al.*, *SIPRI Yearbook 1994* (Oxford University Press: Oxford, 1994), chapter 12, pp. 441–48. Chinese research on the subject includes Wang Shaoguang, 'Demystify China's defense expenditure', unpublished manuscript, 9 May 1995; and Ai Shiuan, 'Yijiujiuerniande zhonggong junshi' [Chinese communist military in 1992], *Zhonggong Yanjiu* [Studies on Chinese Communism Monthly], vol. 27, no. 1 (Jan. 1993), pp. 68–77. Discussions of the complexities and methodological problems involved in calculating China's actual defence spending are found in Bitzinger, R. A., 'Off the books: analyzing and understanding Chinese defense spending', Paper presented at the Fifth Staunton Hill Conference on the PLA, Staunton Hill, Va., 17–19 June 1994; and Shambaugh, D., 'Wealth in search of power: the Chinese military budget and revenue base', Paper presented at the Conference on 'Chinese economic reform: the impact on security policy', Pacific Place Conference Center, Hong Kong, 8–10 July 1994.

[9] Hung P. Nguyen, 'Russia and China: the genesis of an Eastern Rappallo', *Asian Survey*, Mar. 1993, pp. 285–301. Hung P. Nguyen has persuasively argued that Soviet military policy towards China is primarily based on the Soviet need to ally itself with another continental power in the East, as it did with Germany in the 1920s to offset its weakening geopolitical position *vis-à-vis* the West.

border issues.[10] The USSR's efforts culminated in the normalization of relations with China during Gorbachev's visit to Beijing during the Tiananmen Square demonstrations in May 1989.

In the Chinese leadership's view after the Tiananmen crisis, the Soviet emphasis on security was deeply involved with its own concern with internal stability, while the US emphasis on democratic values was seen as part of a 'peaceful evolution' strategy against Communist rule in China. The USSR appeared less threatening to the security and stability of China for the foreseeable future. Another important consideration for the Chinese leadership was that China's preoccupation with economic development necessitated an improvement of relations with neighbouring countries, including its northern neighbour.

II. The resumption of Beijing–Moscow military ties

Military contacts between Beijing and Moscow were resumed, after a 30-year hiatus, within the framework of the political *rapprochement* laid down at the Sino-Soviet summit meeting in May 1989. In addition, the steady development of Sino-Soviet relations in areas such as trade, border issues and high-level visits strengthened their military relationship. Several major political crises, such as the August 1991 coup in Moscow and the disintegration of the Soviet Union, slowed the pace of contacts but did not prevent military ties from becoming firmer. In fact, since 1989 Beijing and Moscow have increased the pace, scope and level of their military cooperation faster than many observers would have thought possible.

Before their high-level military contacts resumed in the summer of 1990, each side had security concerns and suspicions about the other's long-term intentions. Each still maintained a substantial although reduced number of troops on their lengthy border, and the imprint of 30 years of enmity and confrontation was too deep to be washed away in a matter of months.

---

[10] The 'Three Obstacles' as set out by Deng Xiaoping in the early 1980s were: the Soviet occupation of Afghanistan; Soviet support for the Vietnamese occupation of Cambodia; and Soviet troops massed on the Sino-Soviet and Sino-Mongolian borders. For an analysis of the major developments in Sino-Soviet relations leading to the May 1989 summit meeting, see Goldstein, S. M., 'Diplomacy amid protest: the Sino-Soviet summit', *Problems of Communism*, Sep.–Oct. 1989, pp. 49–71.

More importantly, military cooperation with Russia and, in particular, the purchase of Russian weapon systems and technologies posed difficult questions for the Chinese leadership, some of which are not unlike those asked in Beijing during the Sino-Soviet 'honeymoon' of the 1950s. The extensive purchase of Russian arms and military technology would not only be financially undesirable but could also result in a kind of military dependency on Russia. Such dependency has obvious drawbacks for flexibility in China's security policy and, given the faltering state of the Russian defence economy, even brings into question the long-term availability of spare parts and logistics support.

Another fundamental question for China was whether it could expect to receive the most sophisticated weapons and know-how from Russia or whether it would only receive off-the-shelf weapons and/or older technologies. Russia, too, had concerns: Would weapons and technologies transferred today come back to haunt Moscow in the future should security relations with Beijing deteriorate? Despite such uncertainties and risks, both China and Russia apparently decided that political and economic benefits accruing from their military cooperation and arms sales outweighed any negative security implications in the future.

One strong indication of their determination is the frequent contacts between their political and military leaders. Appendix 2 summarizes the reciprocal visits made by ranking Chinese and Soviet/Russian officials related to security relations, military-to-military ties and arms transfers. These areas roughly correspond to the three major components of the Sino-Russian military relationship: (a) troop reduction and military confidence-building measures (MCBMs) along the Sino-Russian border; (b) the long-term development of an institutionalized relationship between the two militaries; and (c) the transfer of Russian weapons and defence technology to China.

The first component of the relationship began immediately after the Sino-Soviet summit meeting in May 1989. It followed two tracks: one for the settlement of perennial border disputes and the other for troop reductions and MCBMs. Regular talks on border settlement, headed by deputy foreign ministers, were held alternately in Beijing and Moscow. In May 1991, both sides formally agreed on the eastern sector of the Sino-Soviet border during General Secretary Jiang Zemin's visit to Moscow. The agreement on the eastern section was ratified by both sides in February 1992,[11] but the disintegration of the Soviet Union in late 1991 had left unresolved the western sector of the former Sino-Soviet border. The western border talks were held by China, Russia and three Central Asian republics (Kazakhstan, Kyrgyzstan and Tajikistan), and an agreement was signed during Jiang Zemin's second visit to Moscow, in September 1994.[12]

Talks on border troop reductions have been coordinated between each side's foreign ministry and military personnel. Thirteen rounds of talks were held between November 1989 and September 1994 on a wide range of issues such as troop relocation, reduction of troops and arms, and MCBMs. By the end of 1993 each side had agreed to withdraw its troops 100 kilometres from the border.[13] The Sino-Russian MCBMs now include the advanced notification of troop movements and exercises and communications links between adjacent military districts.

The second component—the institutionalized military relationship—began in earnest in June 1990 with the reciprocal visits of General Liu Huaqing, Vice-Chairman of the CMC, and Rear Admiral Vladimir Khuzhokov of the Soviet Defence Ministry. Initially aimed at getting acquainted with each other and removing suspicion about the other's intentions, senior military contacts have since broadened the scope of the military relationship. The Chinese and Russian militaries established a network of working relations at various levels: defence ministers exchanged visits, and military chiefs in each service had regular contacts with their counterparts. Military contacts expanded to include provincial-level cooperation, exchange of intelligence delegations and the first-ever reciprocal port calls.[14]

The third component, sales of weapons and defence technology, was at the heart of the new Sino-Russian military relationship. The first discussion on arms sales began during General Liu's June 1990 visit. Not only was this visit the most senior military contact between

---

[11] Tian Zengpei (ed.), *Gaige Kaifang Yilaide Zhongguo Waijiao* [Chinese diplomacy after reform and open-door] (Shijie Zhishi Chubanshe: Beijing, Oct. 1993), pp. 328–29.

[12] FBIS-CHI, 6 Sep. 1994, pp. 10–11.

[13] Russia had most of its troops massed along the Trans-Siberian railway, which was close to the border, while the Chinese troops were stationed well away from the border. China first proposed the demilitarization of an area extending 50 km on either side of the border, which would mean that only the Russian troops would be relocated. The parties later agreed to the demilitarization 'up to 100 kilometres' from the border. The actual relocation, however, has been delayed because of the financial cost.

[14] Gertz, B. 'Russia, China sign pact restoring intelligence ties', *Washington Times*, 21 Oct. 1992, p. A7.

the two sides in decades but both sides, according to Soviet Chief of Staff Mikhail Moiseyev, also agreed on a number of 'principles indispensable for the establishment of mutual relations in the military economic field'. Moiseyev also added that the Soviet Union wanted to have long-term cooperation with China in military technology.[15]

General Liu's visit was followed by extensive and frequent dialogue between the two sides on the transfer of advanced aircraft, missile systems and ground weapons. However, it was Russian First Deputy Defence Minister Andrei Kokoshin's visit to China in October 1992 that led to the Russian agreement to transfer technologies and production rights to China.[16] President Boris Yeltsin could have had in mind Russia's decision to transfer technology to China when he declared during the December 1992 summit meeting that Russia's cooperation would include military high technology. He further emphasized that Russia was 'prepared for cooperation in all fields [with China], including the most sophisticated weapons and armaments'.[17]

The Sino-Russian arms transactions have arisen from somewhat different motives on each side, however. The primary motivation for Russia has been financial. Arms sales generate hard currency for the cash-strapped government and help alleviate economic hardship. They also help protect Russia's defence personnel, industry and technological edge from the devastation wrought by domestic economic and political upheavals. Russia's secondary consideration has been the forging of political relations with customer states and regions.

The Chinese side, on the other hand, has more diverse motivations. At least four major interrelated considerations have been forwarded:

---

[15] 'China seeking Soviet fighters', *Jane's Defence Weekly*, 21 July 1990, p. 70; and 'Soviet chief of general staff on prospects for development of Soviet–Chinese military relations', *Renmin Ribao*, 7 June 1990, p. 4, in FBIS-CHI, 8 June 1990, p. 3.

[16] Andrei Kokoshin's meetings in China included talks with Liu Huaqing and senior officers from the Commission on Science, Technology and Industry for National Defence (COSTIND). He visited several defence factories, including a missile factory in Shanghai. Kokoshin was followed within 2 months by other senior Russian officials who were in charge of defence industrial issues, such as Alexandre Shokhin and V. N. Mykhaylov, and by President Boris Yeltsin. Cheung, T. M., 'Arm in arm', *Far Eastern Economic Review*, 12 Nov. 1992, p. 28. Another report speculated that the Chinese were determined to push for a closer military technological tie with Russia as a reaction to the US sale of 150 F-16s to Taiwan. Spellman, A., 'US, French fighter sales to Taiwan nudge mainland China closer to Russia', *Armed Forces Journal International*, Jan. 1993, p. 16.

[17] FBIS-CHI, 18 Dec. 1992, p. 9, and 21 Dec. 1992, pp. 9–10.

1. China's purchase of Russian weapons and technology was a logical way of correcting the deficiencies of the PLA's huge but largely outdated weapon inventory. This is true partially because of the compatibility between some Russian weaponry and China's current inventory, which is made up almost entirely of systems based on Soviet designs. However, Su-27s and Kilo Class submarines mark an improvement over the older MiGs and Romeo Class submarines of 1950s vintage.

2. Like many other countries, China wished to take advantage of the 'buyer's market' created by the end of the cold war.

3. Chinese arms imports were intended to bolster its military position in Asia, commensurate with its increasing economic and diplomatic status.

4. China possibly hoped to re-export the acquired Russian technologies to other countries in a variety of forms.[18]

Notwithstanding their differing motives at the outset, the balance sheet for their military relationship has been satisfactory to both: China emerged as the largest foreign buyer of Russian weapons in 1992, with purchases worth $1.8 billion.[19] The total cost of China's purchase of Russian weapons and equipment in 1991–94 has been estimated as $4.5–6 billion.[20] According to one report, China has become a most valued customer of the Russian armament exporters and was accorded a special status to negotiate directly with the Russian Defence Ministry, rather than going through state armament export firms under the Ministry of Foreign Economic Relations (MVES) such as Oboroneksport, Spetsvneshtekhnika and, since January 1994, Rosvoorouzhenie. Nevertheless, the negotiations, if they

[18] Hickey, D. V. V. and Harmel, C. C., 'United States and China's military ties with the Russian republics', *Asian Affairs*, vol. 20, no. 4 (winter 1994), pp. 243–47.

[19] President Yeltsin said that Russia's arms sales to China in 1992 amounted to $1.8 billion. *South China Morning Post*, 19 Mar. 1993; and Karniol, R., 'Trade dispute halts Cam Ranh Talks', *Jane's Defence Weekly*, 20 Mar. 1993, p. 12. On the other hand, Prime Minister Yegor Gaidar told the Congress of People's Deputies that arms sales to China during the same period amounted to a value of $1 billion. *Jane's Defence Weekly*, 12 Dec. 1992, p. 10; and FBIS-CHI, 12 Aug. 1992, p. 7.

[20] *Jane's Defence Weekly*, citing a published estimate in Moscow, reported on 19 Nov. 1994 that Russian arms sales to China in 1992–93 were worth $3–5 billion. This estimate does not include the purchase of 4 Kilo Class submarines worth $1–1.5 billion. See also FBIS-SOV, 15 Aug. 1994, pp. 10–11.

t in a decision to export, must be approved at the highest political levels in Russia.[21]

In the end, however, the real long-term success for China depends on its acquisition of Russian production technologies and offset arrangements, which will allow for the increased development of domestic know-how and production capabilities.

III. Actual Soviet and Russian sales

Before discussing specific Sino-Russian arms deals, it is useful to briefly revisit the age-old question of 'self-reliance versus foreign technology'. General Liu Huaqing, China's most senior active-duty military officer, a CCP Politburo Standing Committee member and one of the foremost advocates of Chinese military modernization, has provided guidance to China on how to deal with the problem:

To modernize weapons and equipment, our foothold must be on our own strength. A big developing socialist country like ours cannot buy modernization of the whole [People's Liberation] Army, whereas other countries will not sell us the most advanced things and, even if we can buy those things, we will still be under the control of others . . . When we stress self-reliance, [however] we do not mean we will close the door to pursue our own construction. What we mean is to actively create conditions to import advanced technology from abroad and borrow every useful experience. Military science and technology has no international boundary. One of the basic principles of modernization of weapons and equipment in our Army is to mainly rely on our own strength for regeneration, while selectively importing advanced technology from abroad, centering on some areas.[22]

Under such guidelines, China has sought a wide variety of Russian weapons and technologies but has been relatively cautious in finalizing the deals because of financial and political concerns. Moreover, the Russian side is often unwilling to part with weapons and technologies, and most Chinese wishes go unmet.

---

[21] Martov, A. 'Russia's Asian sales onslaught', *International Defense Review*, May 1994, pp. 49–54, especially p. 49; and Anthony, I., *et al.*, 'The trade in major conventional weapons', *SIPRI Yearbook 1995: Armaments, Disarmament and International Security* (Oxford University Press: Oxford, 1995), pp. 503–505.

[22] Liu Huaqing, 'Unswervingly advance along the road of building a modern army with Chinese characteristics', *Jiefangjun Bao*, 6 Aug. 1993, pp. 1–2, in FBIS-CHI, 18 Aug. 1993, pp. 15–22; the quotation is from p. 19.

Aircraft

In the early 1990s the Chinese military pursued the acquisition of advanced Russian aircraft and related technologies for good reasons. The Air Force is the most technologically oriented service in any country's armed forces, but China's relatively backward aviation industry has long failed to meet PLAAF requirements. Intermittent contacts with Western aircraft manufacturers since the 1970s produced few breakthroughs in either upgrading the existing inventory or developing new generations of fighter aircraft (see chapter 4). As a result, China's most advanced fighter aircraft in production to date has been the Shenyang J-8 II.

In addition, the PLA's strategic shift since the 1985 CMC meeting envisages 'limited local wars' (*youxian jubu zhanzheng*) on border areas as the most likely type of warfare, and this requires rapid mobility and fire power. The PLAAF, however, has been ill-equipped to respond to the new challenges. It is the gap between the doctrinal requirements and the existing aircraft inventory that has sharpened the sense of urgency among the Chinese top brass.

Sino-Soviet negotiations for advanced Soviet aircraft began during General Liu Huaqing's two-week trip to Moscow in June 1990, which included a visit to a Mikoyan aircraft plant.[23] At that time, discussions were focused on the MiG-29 Fulcrum fighter and the Su-24 Fencer ground attack aircraft. By October, Chinese interest shifted to the Su-27 Flanker air-superiority aircraft. China opted for the Su-27 over the MiG-29 mostly for technological and strategic reasons, despite its reported unit cost of $30 million. The Su-27 has a longer range, more advanced avionics and a wider array of mission capabilities than the MiG-29.

The Su-27 Flanker is a high-performance aircraft currently deployed by the Russian Air Force. It is powered by two Saturn AL-31F turbofan engines and has a combat radius of 1500 km. It carries a look-down/shoot-down radar and an infrared search and tracking system and has air-refuelling capabilities. Its armament includes one multi-barrel 30-mm cannon, AA-10 Alamo semi-active radar homing air-to-air missiles (AAMs), AA-8 Aphid and AA-11 Archer

---

[23] General Liu's delegation included Aeronautics and Astronautics Minister Lin Zongtang, Major-General Shen Rongjun, a missile expert and Deputy Director of COSTIND, and Li Lanqing, then Deputy Minster of the Ministry of Foreign Economic Relations and Trade (MOFERT). FBIS-CHI, 1 June 1990, pp. 4–5.

infrared guided AAMs. The Su-27 is comparable to the F-15 in performance and mission capability. However, some reports indicate that the Su-27s provided to China may not include the AA-10 and AA-11 missiles and may have an older-generation electronic countermeasures pod on board.[24]

The final deal was believed to be concluded during Soviet Defence Minister Dmitri Yazov's visit to Beijing in May 1991, a full year after General Liu's visit to Moscow. China acquired 24 Su-27s, as well as 144 AA-10 AAMs, 96 AA-8 AAMs, 40 spare engines and a Su-27 flight simulator. It is believed that China bought two additional Su-27UB trainers at the end of 1992, bringing the total to 26. The final cost, including the aircraft, armament, spare engines and training support, has been estimated at $1.3–1.5 billion.[25]

In the period 1991–93 China also imported military transport aircraft to enhance its airlift capability. Under a contract signed in 1990, China took delivery in 1991 of two dozen Mi-17 transport helicopters.[26] In 1992 and 1993 China further acquired 10 Il-76M heavy transport aircraft.[27] In 1993, under mysterious circumstances, China may have also swapped a huge amount of canned fruit for an ageing Il-28 bomber/transport.

Since the Su-27 deal, numerous unconfirmed reports pointed to possible follow-on sales of various Mikoyans and Sukhois, namely,

[24] On the Su-27, see Lake, J., *Sukhoi Su-27 'Flanker'* (Aerospace Publishing: London, 1994). See also Zaloga, S. J. 'Current trends in Russian aviation missiles', *The Future of the Russian Air Force, Jane's Intelligence Review* special report no. 4 (Sep. 1994), pp. 21–24; and Zaloga, S. J., 'Russian missile designations', *Jane's Intelligence Review*, Aug. 1994, pp. 342–49. On the delivery of less-advanced sub-systems with the Su-27, see Cheung, T. M., 'Ties of convenience: Sino-Russian military relations in the 1990s', ed. R. H. Yang, *China's Military: The PLA in 1992/1993* (Westview Press: Boulder, Colo., 1993), p. 66; and Ryan, S. L., 'The PLA Navy's search for a blue water capability', *Asian Defense Journal*, May 1994, p. 32.

[25] Cheung (note 24), p. 61; and Pinkov (Ping Kefu), *The Analysis of Current Status of Talks on Arms Reduction in the Border Area and Arms Trade between Russia and China* (Kanwa Translation Information Centre Canada: Toronto, Aug. 1994), pp. 4–5.

[26] The scheduled delivery of 10 Mi-17 helicopters and 3 Il-76s was revealed by Soviet Minister of Foreign Economic Relations K. Katushev in an interview. See *Jingji Ribao*, 21 Apr. 1990, p. 1, in FBIS-CHI, 3 May 1990, pp. 3–4. See also *South China Morning Post*, 9 Nov. 1992, and appendix 1 in this volume.

[27] The official Xinhua (New China) News Agency reported in Sep. 1991 that China had ordered 3 Il-76TDs in Oct. 1990 and that their delivery had been arranged by China National Machinery Import and Export Corporation. See FBIS-CHI, 27 Sep. 1991, p. 18. Tai Ming Cheung reported in 1993, however, that Polytechnologies, the arms trading company of the PLA General Staff Department, purchased 7 Il-76s for $200 million with 40% in hard currency and the rest in barter goods. See Cheung, T. M., 'Arms reduction', *Far Eastern Economic Review*, 14 Oct. 1993, p. 68.

the MiG-29s, MiG-31s, Su-30s and Su-35s.[28] Given the extent of Sino-Russian air force contacts, including several air exhibitions held in Beijing and Moscow, it is reasonable to assume that Russia has provided China with detailed information on various kinds of advanced aircraft. The PLA's financial constraints, however, effectively ruled out the importation of the Russian aircraft in massive numbers. As of December 1994, none of the MiG sales to China has been confirmed, and several Russian officials have on various occasions denied the reports that MiG sales or production arrangements have been made.[29]

A potentially more important transfer was the Chinese contract in 1992 with NPO Klimov to import 100 Klimov/Sarkisov RD-33 turbofan engines, which power the MiG-29. China reportedly secured the latest model, the RD-33K, and all engines had been delivered to China by the end of 1993.[30] Analysts believe that they would power Chinese fighters nearing production or under development.

In 1992–93 China also placed an order for the second batch of 26 Su-27 aircraft, whose production had been completed by early 1994. Its delivery was delayed by unresolved issues such as payment terms and the transfer of technology and production equipment.[31] Russia insisted that 70 per cent or more of the payment be made in hard currency, compared to 35 per cent for the first batch of Su-27s in 1992.

According to some reports, China has shown an interest in obtaining the licence for local production of a number of advanced aircraft, including the Su-27 and the Su-35. The Su-35 is a highly advanced

[28] Some exaggerated press reports argued that China purchased the MiG-29s or MiG-31s in 1992, while others cited China's purchase or co-production of as many as 300 MiGs. See WuDunn, S., 'China shops for Russian aircraft carrier', *International Herald Tribune*, 8 June 1992, pp. 1–2; Sengupta, P., 'China expands air forces', *Military Technology*, Aug. 1992 pp. 49–50; Dantes, E., 'The PLA air force build-up: an appraisal', *Asian Defence Journal*, Nov. 1992, pp. 42–48; and Davis, M. R., 'Russia's big arms sales drive', *Asia–Pacific Defence Reporter*, Aug.–Sep. 1994, pp. 11–12.

[29] In a Mar. 1994 interview with a Hong Kong correspondent, Gregory S. Logvinov, Director of the China Bureau of the Russian Foreign Ministry, confirmed China's purchase of the first batch of 26 Su-27s and the ongoing negotiations for an additional 26 Su-27s, but denied that any MiG-29s or MiGs-31 had been sold to China. See Pinkov (Ping Kefu) (note 25). Discussions held in 1993 and 1994 by the present authors with officials from Russian arms export companies and with high-ranking members of the Russian Foreign Ministry, responsible for relations with China, also confirm that no follow-on transfers or co-production deals are in the offing other than the continuing negotiations on a second shipment of Su-27s.

[30] 'Sino-Russian talks on carrier-based aircraft', *International Defense Review*, Sep. 1994, p. 13.

[31] *Jane's Defence Weekly*, 22 Jan. 1994, p. 3.

version of the Su-27, which has yet to enter service in the Russian Air Force. According to Mikhail Simonov, head of the Sukhoi Design Bureau, the Su-35 is a significant upgrade of the Su-27 with a variety of new features, including thrust-vectored engines, a rearward-facing air interception radar and new digital fly-by-wire controls.[32] The Sukhoi bureau officials reportedly proposed the co-production of the Su-35 in China, on condition that China purchase up to 120 Su-35s, and a Western defence correspondent reported in mid-1995 that the two sides had reached an agreement in principle to begin Chinese licensed production of perhaps as many as 100 Su-27s a year.[33]

In spite of much speculation, however, by mid-1995 no co-production deal had materialized or been confirmed. The purchase price for such a large number of advanced aircraft would be a towering barrier for China, and it remains unclear whether such deals can be approved in Moscow, even in the light of the declining orders for MiGs and Sukhois from either Russian or foreign air forces. While there is no doubt that China wants to obtain such aircraft, financial, political and security concerns have more often than not weighed against the conclusion of such deals.

Naval systems and equipment

China's rapid economic development in the 1980s has significantly increased the importance of protecting its maritime interests in overall national security and development planning. Continuing prosperity in the Special Economic Zones (SEZs) and in the open cities along its long eastern seaboard is crucial for the success of China's reform programme. Since the mid-1980s, moreover, China has begun to emphasize a new naval strategy called 'offshore active defence', in line with the PLA's new defence strategy.[34] China's maritime interests now

[32] Su-35 "as capable as EFA or Rafale"', *Jane's Defence Weekly*, 12 Sep. 1992, p. 7; and 'Su-35 to have "over the shoulder" ability', *Jane's Defence Weekly*, 20 Feb. 1993, p. 6. For Taiwan's assessment of the impact of Su-35 purchases by China, see FBIS-CHI, 17 Oct. 1994, p. 14.

[33] Boey, D., 'Chinese may choose Su-35 over MiG-29', *Defense News*, 28 Mar.–3 Apr. 1994; and 'Made in China deal is forged for Su-27s', *Jane's Defence Weekly*, 6 May 1995, p. 3. Gennady Yanpolsky, Vice-Chairman of the State Committee for Defense Sectors of Industry, insisted that Russia intends to sell the Su-27 and the Su-30 but not the more advanced Su-35. FBIS-SOV, 10 Aug. 1994, p. 11.

[34] For an analysis of China's new naval doctrine, see Huang, A. C., 'The Chinese Navy's offshore active defense strategy: conceptualization and implications', *Naval War College Review*, summer 1994, pp. 7–32.

include the safeguarding of China's territorial waters, coastal economy, seaborne trade and maritime resources, deterring Taiwan independence, and maintaining strategic depth. Liu Huaqing put it clearly:

It is imperative to establish a powerful and modern navy. The three main tasks of the people's navy [PLAN] are to safeguard the motherland's sacred territorial waters, to counterattack hegemonists and advocates of power politics who play with fire and dare to invade our country, and to accomplish the great cause of the reunification of the motherland and smash all attempts to break China up by practising 'Taiwan independence' and 'one China, one Taiwan'.[35]

However, despite China's growing maritime interests and the potential to receive Russian naval equipment, actual transactions in this area have been modest. The foremost reason has been that China is itself a major shipbuilder which produces a wide array of military vessels. Reports in 1993 indicated that China was likely to overtake South Korea as the world's second largest shipbuilder.[36] In the early 1990s, for example, China's shipyards rolled out various new models and classes of vessel: the Luhu (Type-052) guided-missile destroyer, the Jiangwei (Type-055) guided-missile frigate, Houxin and Houjian fast attack craft, Huludao coastal patrol craft, the Dayun resupply ship and new amphibious assault ships.[37] For this reason, China's interests in Russia's naval equipment and technology have focused on the latter's assistance in power projection capability, such as aircraft-carriers, submarines and possibly naval weapons. Despite a considerable increase in naval contacts in 1993–94, there has been only one major naval contract between China and Russia—regarding the sale of submarines.

The long-discussed Kilo Class submarine sale was concluded during Russian Navy Commander Felix Gromov's visit to China in November 1994 to discuss 'military–technological cooperation between the two sides'.[38] The contract is believed to be for four Type-877EKM Kilo Class submarines at about $250 million each. The original submarine package offered by Rosvoorouzhenie, the

---

[35] Liu quoted in British Broadcasting Corporation, *Summary of World Broadcasts: Far East*, FE/1607, 8 Feb. 1993, p. A2/4.

[36] See British Broadcasting Corporation, *Summary of World Broadcasts: Far East*, FE/W0268, 10 Feb. 1993, p. A/5.

[37] 'Chasing the 20th century', *Jane's Defence Weekly*, 19 Feb. 1994, pp. 26–27; and Karniol, R., 'China's new navy takes shape', *Jane's Defence Weekly*, 6 June 1992, p. 958.

[38] FBIS-SOV, 1 Nov. 1994, p. 10; and FBIS-CHI, 8 Nov. 1994, pp. 11–12.

state armament trading corporation, reportedly included six Kilo Class submarines, a simulator, accompanying base infrastructure and an 18-month training programme.[39] Although the total number of submarines in this sale was reduced to four, it is likely that the sale still meets Russian quantitative requirements for technology transfer. Reports at the time by US naval sources state that China agreed to purchase 10 Kilo Class submarines and may purchase an additional 12.[40]

The negotiation over the Kilo Class submarines began during the April 1993 trip to Russia by PLA Navy Commander Zhang Lianzhong, who is a submarine officer himself. Admiral Zhang's visit was followed two months later by Deputy Naval Commander He Pengfei, who was accompanied to Russia by submarine experts from Wuhan.[41] China's interest in acquiring the Russian Kilo submarines stems from the fact that, despite the PLA's full inventory of over 100 submarines, half of them are non-operational and ageing Romeo Class submarines. A newer version, the improved Ming Class submarine, has increasingly spent long maintenance hours at the docks and is based on decades-old designs and technology.

The Kilo Class submarines would be a significant addition to China's ageing submarine fleet. The Kilo submarine is diesel-electric powered and is designed for both anti-surface and anti-submarine warfare (ASW) roles. With a maximum submerged speed of 17 knots and cruising range of 9500 km, it has an endurance of 45 days under the surface with a crew of 51. The 877EKM version which China is believed to have ordered is the export model and includes an upgraded fire-control system and wire-guided torpedoes, improvements over the basic Kilo model.[42] The Kilo Class submarines are likely to be assigned to China's South and East Fleets and would be ideal for the PLAN's mission to safeguard the Chinese-claimed territorial waters in the South China Sea and possibly to impose a naval

---

[39] Karniol, R., 'China to buy Russian "Kilo" submarines', *Jane's Defence Weekly*, 19 Nov. 1994, p. 1.

[40] See Starr, B., 'China's SSK aspirations detailed by USN chief', *Jane's Defence Weekly*, 18 Mar. 1995, p. 3.

[41] Cheung, T. M., 'China's buying spree', *Far Eastern Economic Review*, 8 July 1993, pp. 24, 26.

[42] For technical presentation of Oboroneksport's defence products, including the Kilo submarine, see 'Defence products from Russia', *Military Technology*, Feb. 1993, pp. 40–47. On the Kilo, see also Sharpe, R. (ed.), *Jane's Fighting Ships, 1994–95* (Jane's Information Group: Coulsdon, Surrey, 1994), p. 541.

blockade in the Taiwan Strait. The first submarine to be delivered was sighted leaving St Petersburg bound for China aboard a transport ship in March 1995.[43]

Much speculation and media attention were devoted to China's possible interest in acquiring the 67 500-tonne *Varyag*, a sister ship of the carrier *Kuznetsov*, which was being fitted out in Ukraine after the demise of the USSR.[44] The purchase of a foreign-made aircraft-carrier is not a viable option at present, however: China faces no immediate maritime threat and practical obstacles to acquiring an aircraft-carrier persist—the astronomical purchase price, lack of special equipment, training and defence—not to mention the probable diplomatic and military repercussions of China's acquiring such offensive capability. By all accounts, China's interest in purchasing a foreign-made aircraft-carrier has declined somewhat. However, a desire for the eventual development of a carrier force remains strong.[45]

In sum, as a major shipbuilder, China is likely to rely on its own technology and know-how to build most of its naval vessels. However, cooperation with the Russian military will be a significant factor in fulfilling China's blue-water ambitions. In particular, China is likely to find the Russian connection useful in providing components and sub-systems for Chinese naval hulls. Also, Russia might provide aircraft-carrier technology, such as steam catapult systems, defence systems and naval aircraft. Looking ahead, it seems that there will be continued cooperation in the naval sphere. During Russian Navy Commander Felix Gromov's 1994 visit to China, topics of discussion included the provision of Russian naval personnel to train Chinese officers and crews.[46]

Land systems

Several press reports indicated that China purchased 50 T-72 MBTs and 70 armoured vehicles at a cost of about $250 million, in addition to a large number of old T-62s from Russia for scrap, but these

[43] Starr (note 40).

[44] *Jane's Defence Weekly*, 8 Feb. and 29 Aug. 1992.

[45] For China's continuing interest in building aircraft carriers, see Lu Ti, 'China's progress in secretly building aircraft carrier', *Chien Shao* (Hong Kong), 8 May 1994, pp. 20–23, in FBIS-CHI, 10 May 1994, pp. 16–19; and Li Yuling, *Zhongguo Haijun Shili* [Chinese naval power] (Kuang Chiao Ching: Hong Kong, June 1993), pp. 155–64.

[46] FBIS-CHI, 8 Nov. 1994, p. 11.

reports were unconfirmed at this writing.[47] In general, land systems have received the least attention in the Sino-Russian arms agenda. China's apparent lack of interest in acquiring Russian land systems has to do with budgetary and strategic considerations. The PLA ground force is 2.2 million strong and has a massive inventory of ground weapons. Its own defence industry is vastly underutilized, employing only a small percentage of its full capacity to roll out the latest versions of land systems, such as T-85/T-85 II MBTs and WM-80 multiple launch rockets (MLRs). Chinese military planners apparently concluded not only that the size and armaments of the PLA are adequate to meet any land attack but also that the prospects for land attack are slim, with traditional land-based threats to China significantly reduced in the post-cold war period.

In addition, limited defence funds need to be allocated for a few select units and purposes. China's remaining interest in Russia's land systems will be to equip the 'fist units' (*quantou budui*). These rapid reaction units (RRUs) were created in each of the seven MRs in the late 1980s. The RRUs, specially trained for different geographical and climatic conditions, were geared to strengthen mobility and operational coordination in preparation for small-scale warfare on and around China's border areas. The recent spread of RRUs in the PLA's order-of-the-battle, by upgrading three brigades of the 15th Airborne Army to full divisions, also indicates a potential area for future Russian sales in limited quantities.[48]

Air-defence missile systems

In March 1993 China took delivery of a Russian S-300PMU SA-10 'Grumble' air-defence missile system, with a total of 100 missiles. The S-300PMU system has an engagement range of 90 km and, in principle, is capable of intercepting both incoming missiles and aircraft, depending on the type of missile used. The system was, however, originally developed to engage enemy aircraft and has a limited effectiveness in intercepting long-range missiles.

Moreover, the number of missiles purchased by China is too small to provide an effective air defence for major cities such as Beijing and

[47] FBIS-CHI, 14 July 1993, p. 7. There are also unconfirmed reports that China ordered 400 T-72 MBTs from Russia in 1992. See FBIS-CHI, 5 May 1992, p. 5.

[48] *Jane's Defence Weekly*, 2 Oct. 1993, p. 12.

Tianjin; they will be a supplement to the Chinese RF-61A SAM designed to engage incoming targets at low altitude. At least part of the imported system will be used for testing and research purposes, especially guidance and radar systems. The S-300PMU incorporates phased-array radar technology and a multi-target combat system, which might be utilized to improve Chinese Second Artillery Forces' early-warning system.[49] Some Western sources reported in early 1994 that China was negotiating with the Moscow-based Almaz Design Bureau to purchase a more advanced S-300 system.[50] A further purchase of S-300 systems is likely.

Transfer of technology and production rights

Unlike the past sale of weapons off-the-shelf, the transfer of technologies usually entails a more long-term and sustained commitment from both sides. It also indicates more intimate military relations. While the secretive and ongoing nature of the process does not allow the analyst to make a definitive statement on each technology transfer, available sources indicate that the transfer of aviation technology has been an important aspect of the Sino-Russian military dialogue.

The Chinese contract for 100 RD-33 turbofan engines is believed to have involved an agreement to produce the aircraft engine jointly with Russia for a new-generation Chinese fighter, perhaps the made-for-export Super-7. According to one report, Russia has agreed to transfer technology gradually on 'each stage of production until China can produce the engine all by itself'.[51] Another source, citing Sukhoi Design Bureau officials, revealed that China has officially requested production rights for the Saturn AL-31F turbofan engine, which powers the Su-27.[52] China purchased 40 AL-31F engines for spares as part of the Su-27 acquisition in 1992.

While speculation abounds, the talks on co-production of advanced MiG and Sukhoi aircraft seemed to have made only modest progress. At the least, the first batch of Su-27s involved no technology transfer,

[49] Tseng Hui-yen, 'Russia delivers five sets of missiles to Mainland China', *Lien Ho Pao* (Hong Kong), 20 Oct. 1993, p. 10, in FBIS-CHI, 20 Oct. 1993, p. 9.

[50] '"Flanker" sale stalls as China seeks new deal', *Jane's Defence Weekly*, 22 Jan. 1994, p. 3.

[51] Cited in Pinkov (Ping Kefu) (note 25), p. 4.

[52] 'Sino-Russian talks on carrier-based aircraft', *International Defense Review*, Sep. 1994, p. 13.

according to the well-known first chief test pilot of the Su-27, Major General Vladimir Ilyushin, of the Sukhoi Design Bureau. He added, however, that 'export of [Su-27] technology is still under negotiation'.[53] On balance, China's order for additional Su-27s could mean that any MiG purchase is unlikely in the near future. A more likely course would be that China requests co-production rights for the Su-27, or its advanced version, the Su-35, on the grounds that a total of 50–52 Sukhoi fighters might meet a quantity requirement for technology transfer.

The Chinese purchase of Russian Kilo Class submarines at the end of 1994 may include related submarine technologies. China has for years tried to overcome several specific technological difficulties associated with submarines and surface combatants, such as noise, propulsion systems, periscope technology and torpedoes. In particular, noise problems make PLAN submarines vulnerable to ASW capabilities, such as those possessed by Taiwan. Troubles abounded in the production of the Ming Class submarine, with only nine produced between 1971 and 1994 and with no new vessels appearing between 1979 and 1987.[54] In August 1994 China's commissioning of a new type of diesel-electric submarine, the Wuhan-C, prompted some security analysts to believe that China preferred indigenous production to importation of foreign technology.[55] China's acquisition of the Kilo Class submarine, however, suggests China's continuing interest in foreign naval technology. Seen from this perspective, the Kilo deal could well be a significant boost to PLAN's war-fighting capability and submarine technology.

However, China's efforts to acquire advanced technology from Russia can take other paths as well. One such path has been the transfer of dual-use technologies. In April 1994, for example, Moscow announced the establishment of a joint venture firm with China.[56] The company will reconfigure the designs of existing electro-optic defence items to make commercial laser and optical devices.

[53] FBIS-CHI, 20 Oct. 1992, pp. 2–3.

[54] Sharpe (note 42), p. 115

[55] Starr, B., 'USN fears growth in nuclear Chinese Navy', *Jane's Defence Weekly*, 7 Jan. 1995, p. 6.

[56] Beaver, P., 'Russian industry feels the cold', *Jane's Defence Weekly*, 7 May 1994, p. 30. According to Igor Rogachev, Russian Ambassador to China, at the end of 1992 over 2000 Russian enterprises had been granted the right to sell directly to China. See FBIS-SOV, 13 Jan. 1993, pp. 24–25. See also Sorokin, K., 'Russia's "new look" arms sales strategy', *Arms Control Today*, Oct. 1993, pp. 7–12.

Another area of intensive Sino-Russian dialogue has been that of missile systems. China has been interested in improving its missile systems through Russia's advanced technologies. One indication is the number of Chinese missile experts who shuttled between Beijing and Moscow, including Vice-Director of COSTIND Major General Shen Rongjun (June 1990) and Deputy Commander of the Second Artillery Corps Qian Gui (August 1991). The potential areas for cooperation include missile guidance systems, testing equipment and cruise missiles.[57]

In addition, China has reportedly recruited a number of Russian scientists and engineers in nuclear and missile research and has responded favourably to Russia's proposals for regular and close reciprocal exchanges of information and scientific personnel. One estimate held that in 1993 there were over 1000 Russian scientific personnel working at various institutes under the Chinese Aeronautics Ministry.[58] The same Russian sources acknowledged that a few hundred Chinese defence scientists were then working at Russian research institutes.

To sum up, the prospects for Sino-Russian cooperation in the field of defence technology have improved in recent years. One further indication of this trend was the five-year agreement on military cooperation signed during Russian Defence Minister Pavel Grachev's visit to China in November 1993. While the agreement is not public, it reportedly covers not only weapon sales but also cooperation in the technical field and in personnel exchanges, training and mutual logistic support.[59]

IV. Conclusions

A fortuitous combination of economic and strategic changes in both China and the USSR in the late 1980s presented an opportunity for the two countries to resume military ties. The above review of military contacts indicates that China is likely to seek more weapons and military technologies from Russia in the coming years but that a number of financial, political and security considerations on both sides will place limits on the quantity and quality of those transfers.

[57] Gordon, M., 'Russian sales fuel arms race', *International Herald Tribune*, 19 Oct. 1992.

[58] Cheung (note 41), pp. 24, 26; and 'Asia scared about expansion of Russo-Chinese military cooperation', *Izvestiya*, 9 Nov. 1993, pp. 1, 3, in FBIS-CHI, 10 Nov. 1993, pp. 10–11.

[59] FBIS-CHI, 15 Nov. 1993, p. 13; and FBIS-SOV, 15 Aug. 1994, pp. 10–11.

Table 3.1. Actual and potential transfers of major conventional weapons and military-related items from the Soviet Union/Russia to China, 1990–95

Weapon type	Year(s) of delivery	Number	Comments
Actual transfers			
Mi-17 helicopter	1990–91	24	For transport
Su-27 fighter	1992	26	An additional 26 on order
AA-8 missile	1991–92	96	For Su-27s
AA-10 missile	1991–92	144	For Su-27s
SA-10 SAM	1993	100	With 4 launching systems
Il-76 transport	1992–93	10	For troop transport
Il-28 bomber	1993	1	Exchanged for canned fruit
RD-33 engine	1993	100	For Super-7 fighters
Kilo Class submarine	1995	1	3 more on delivery with more transfers possible
Potential transfers			
Combat aircraft	. .	. .	Under negotiation for possible co-production
Avionics, engines, airframes	. .	. .	Under negotiation
T-72 MBT	. .	. .	Under negotiation
Submarine and ASW technology	. .	. .	Under negotiation

Sources: See appendix 1 in this volume. See also *Jane's Defence Weekly*, 19 Feb. 1994, pp. 26–28, 30–31; *Defense News*, 28 Mar.–3 Apr. and 18–24 Apr. 1994; *Far Eastern Economic Review*, 3 Sep. 1992, p. 21, and 8 July 1993, pp. 24, 26; Pinkov (Ping Kefu), *The Analysis of Current Status of Talks on Arms Reduction in the Border Area and Arms Trade Between Russia and China* (Kanwa Translation Information Centre: Toronto, Aug. 1994), pp. 1–7; and the SIPRI arms trade database, 1995.

Russia's actual transfers to China, and potential transfers under negotiation, are shown in table 3.1.

In the light of its technological difficulties in producing an advanced combat aircraft, it is likely that China will concentrate on acquiring various aerospace technologies and production rights from Russia in the coming years. China's interest probably lies in aerospace items such as avionics systems, aircraft engines, and technical data for the design and construction of airframes. China's security planners may well believe that past failures in air force modernization have left few alternatives and that further delay in this area could cost

China's growing national interests dear. China's acquisition c. Su-27s in particular and its aerospace cooperation with Russia seem to have been informed by this sense of urgency.

Of particular interest in this regard is the outcome of the current negotiation for the second batch of Su-27s, a deal held up owing to disagreements over payment terms and technology transfer issues. China's priority has been to develop an advanced indigenous fighter, with initial Russian (and Israeli) technological assistance. However, Chinese military leaders have not yet secured the requisite technologies, whether for the J-10, Su-27, Su-35 or a new, next-generation aircraft. An informed source noted that in the joint aircraft development project Russia would provide two-thirds of the technical input and design, as well as avionics and engines, for a Chinese next-generation fighter, while China would bear the initial start-up costs of an estimated $500 million.[60] If the joint aircraft project materializes as described, this could lay a solid ground for China's air force modernization.

On the other side of the border, the Russian Federation's continuing economic difficulties and domestic instabilities have created strong pressures to sell weapons overseas. Since the last days of the Soviet Union, state funding of defence production has been declining precipitously. According to the latest Russian official report, Russia's 1994 defence budget allocated funding for the production of only 17 aircraft, and a mere 7 per cent of the naval shipbuilding programme received adequate funding.[61] In addition, the Russian Government's State Committee for the Defence Industry (Roskomoboronprom) reported that defence R&D appropriation for 1994 was only about 2.4 trillion roubles (less than $1 billion), and the figure for 1995 was to be 30 per cent less.[62] This means that Russian defence manufacturers must find sources for their own R&D funding, probably by adopting an aggressive overseas market strategy.

---

[60] Cheung (note 41), pp. 24, 26. The Mikoyan and Sukhoi aircraft manufacturers have long competed for not only aircraft sales but also a variety of aviation deals with China in such areas as the Super-7 and F-8 upgrade, aircraft engines and the next-generation fighter. The Sukhois are leading the competition, but the sale of RD-33 engines, which power the MiG-29s, opened the potential for Mikoyan's upgrade of various Chinese aircraft, the majority of which are MiG derivatives.

[61] Beaver (note 56), p. 30.

[62] 'Rosvoorouzhenie funds new projects', *International Defense Review*, Nov. 1994, pp. 66–67.

In recent years, Russia has pushed the Thai and South Korean Governments hard to accept Russian weapons and weapon technology to compensate for debts it owed or inherited from the Soviet Union.[63] In the Thai case, Russia proposed military helicopters to clear a $65 million debt for its rice imports. The Russian Government has also allegedly offered a reference list for weapons to the Chinese side to resolve the growing debt problem.[64]

Certain potential difficulties should be considered against these positive indications for Russian arms and arms technology exports to China. In military aircraft, continued Sino-Russian cooperation may depend on the outcome of current Sino-Israeli cooperation to develop a new-generation Chinese fighter.[65] In addition, certain influential voices in Russia urge caution in cooperating with China in the military sphere, arguing that this presents a risk to Russia's long-term interests.[66] Moreover, in Russia, the arms manufacturers are often displeased with the arrangements made by Rosvoorouzhenie and the Moscow politcal and military leadership, finding that working with China is cumbersome and unprofitable. Also, Sino-Russian agreements to limit the amount of barter involved in arms deals may well place limits on the amount of equipment China is prepared to acquire.

If the current level of Sino-Russian military cooperation can be sustained—and this is not a forgone conclusion—the relationship could have a significant long-term effect on the PLA's overall defence modernization. At a minimum, Russia has provided China with access to weapon systems and select technologies that have not been available to China in earlier decades. The PLA, on its part, seems eager to reap the benefits of newly developed Sino-Russian military links by focusing on the acquisition of technology and production rights.

---

[63] FBIS-SOV, 10 Aug 1994, p. 9.

[64] Chou Te-hui, 'Russia supplies Beijing with an arms sales list', *Lien Ho Pao* (Hong Kong), 26 Apr. 1994, p. 2, in FBIS-CHI, 26 Apr. 1994, p. 18.

[65] See chapter 4, section III in this volume for a discussion of Sino-Israeli cooperation.

[66] See FBIS-SOV, 16 Nov. 1994, p. 10.

4. Contemporary Chinese arms and technology imports from the West and the developing world

For a big country such as China, relying on the purchase of weapons and equipment will not do to realize defence modernization. It is not just a question of price . . . even 'highly sensitive' defence high technology cannot be bought even if one wants to buy it. . . . Only based on one's own skill and talents can imports be digested and absorbed, and technology transfer take place. (From the official history of the Chinese defence science and technology sector, 1992[1])

I. Introduction

The aftermath of the 1989 Tiananmen Square crisis dealt a serious blow to China's efforts to import military-use items from the West. However, since 1990 China has significantly expanded the extent of its foreign contacts in military affairs. These contacts have included high-level discussions related to arms imports in spite of the post-Tiananmen sanctions and isolation. The main suppliers involved in the trade of military hardware and technology appear to have been Russia and Israel, although other suppliers—including France, Germany, Iran, Italy, Pakistan, the UK and the USA—have offered technologies and equipment which have potential military applications.

The Chinese Ministry of Defence reported that in 1992 alone the PLA received 110 military delegations from more than 40 countries, including 11 defence ministers, and that the PLA sent more than 70 delegations to 20 countries in that year. The official Xinhua News Agency reported that the PLA Air Force had the largest number of personnel visiting abroad in its history in 1992—foreign contacts which assisted in training, weaponry and equipment development, formulation of strategy and tactics, and scientific research.[2]

---

[1] Xie Guang *et al.* (eds), *Dangdai Zhongguo de Guofang Keji Shiye* [Modern China's science and technological undertakings in national defence], vol. 2 (Dangdai Zhongguo Chubanshe: Beijing, 1992), pp. 492–93 (authors' translation).

[2] 'China seeks to renew military links', *International Herald Tribune*, 30 July 1993, p. 2; and 'Air force increases international exchanges', Xinhua, 19 Feb. 1993, in British Broad-

In the first six months of 1993, the PLA sent delegations to some 40 countries and received about 50 delegations from around 20 countries. In 1994 the PLA received 122 delegations with over 2000 people from 57 countries and sent some 58 delegations to 62 foreign countries. The official Chinese news agency noted that visits in 1994 were characterized in part by an increase in the proportion of visits by the PLA aimed at 'promoting professional and technological exchanges and cooperation with foreign counterparts'.[3] In 1995 a number of Western military leaders visited China.[4]

A number of factors can be cited to explain these developments. As discussed in chapter 3, the collapse of the Soviet Union led to improved Sino-Russian relations while at the same time compelling the post-Soviet arms industry to find export markets in China. With the imposition of post-Tiananmen sanctions against China by the West, Beijing was able to turn its improved relations with the Soviet Union to its advantage. Indeed, one report noted that within only days of the Tiananmen crackdown, the Chinese leadership made approaches to Moscow for access to technologies and financial support to replace those expected to be lost from the West.[5] The collapse of the Soviet Union also removed the principal strategic motivation behind Western, and especially US, transfers of weapons and technologies to China, so that China had to turn elsewhere. China's purchases of aircraft from the Soviet Union in the early 1990s can in part be explained by the cancellation of the US Chinook helicopter deal as well as the annulment of the J-8II upgrade and the Super-7 development programmes.

For similar reasons, China also turned to Israel to acquire weapons and technologies that were unavailable from the West. This ongoing and clandestine relationship received a boost with the normalization of relations between Israel and China in January 1992, allowing for more open and extensive military ties between the two countries. For

casting Corporation, *Summary of World Broadcasts: Far East* (hereafter cited as *SWB: Far East*), FE/1623, 26 Feb. 1993, p. B2/5.

[3] 'China extends its exchange visits', *Jane's Defence Weekly*, 23 Oct. 1993, p. 15; and '"Unprecedented" level of contacts with foreign armies in 1994', in British Broadcasting Company, *SWB: Far East*, FE/2193, 5 Jan. 1995, p. G/2. See also 'Seoul, Beijing to expand military ties', *Newsreview* (Seoul), 4 Mar. 1995, p. 11.

[4] 'Taboo fading, China and West mend military ties', *International Herald Tribune*, 24 Mar. 1995, p. 4.

[5] 'China seeks aid from Soviets to replace West losses', *Washington Times*, 30 June 1989, p. 11.

Western suppliers, the passage of time since June 1989 has allowed them to move tentatively, but incrementally, back into the Chinese market. From a Chinese perspective, the arms and weapon technology import programme of the 1990s is driven by an increasing availability of resources for military budgets, the improved political position of military modernizers, uneasiness about the nation's strategic future, and increased efforts to look for friends and allies.

With these points providing a background, this chapter reviews developments since 1989 regarding Chinese weapons and technology acquisitions from the United States and other Western suppliers, as well as from Iran, Israel and Pakistan.

II. Western sources of supply

The United States

The major Sino-US military production cooperation agreements reached in the late 1980s were suspended or cancelled during or soon after the Tiananmen crackdown, and no direct sales of complete weapon platforms or weapon production assistance has since been initiated. In May 1994, President Clinton extended sanctions banning US arms and technology deliveries to China. However, the trend since 1992 has been towards liberalization of US policy regarding technology transfers to China, although relations concerning military-related transfers were generally cool and cautious and certainly did not reach the level of closeness that the two sides experienced in the 1980s. Arguments have been presented in both China and the USA in favour of renewing the military cooperation relationship, and some steps (short of arms transfers) have been taken since 1993.

Development of the US Peace Pearl Program continued briefly after June 1989 but was cancelled in April 1990 by China, owing to escalating costs and unsatisfactory delivery times resulting from the decision by the US Department of Defense not to release the complete avionics kits to China until some undetermined date in the future.[6] Some production equipment related to the munitions modernization programme had been transferred to China, but the final production plant had not been opened when the programme was suspended in

---

[6] 'China terminates F-8II upgrade with USAF', *Defence*, July 1990, p. 422; and interview with PLA Air Force colonel involved with the Peace Pearl Program, Oct. 1994.

June 1989. Two out of four sets of artillery-locating radar had been shipped to China in 1988, with the shipment of the other two suspended. Some test equipment and other items related to the Mk46 torpedo programme had been delivered before 1989, but the torpedoes themselves had not been shipped when the programme was suspended.[7] Similarly, the Grumman–CATIC agreement to develop the Super-7 fighter was cancelled, and the planned shipment of six CH47D Chinook helicopters, under an agreement reached in March 1989, was suspended. The Jaguar MBT development programme continued without Chinese participation (these programmes are discussed in greater detail in chapter 3).

However, beginning in the closing weeks of the Bush Administration and gathering pace during much of the Clinton Administration, US policy on military relations with China made some progress, including the transfer of military-related technology. On 22 December 1992, the State Department announced that the USA would return equipment to China under the four US Foreign Military Sales programmes. The decision covered the reimbursement of unused funds in the Chinese FMS account, the shipment of items which China had bought as part of the FMS agreements and the return of Chinese equipment brought to the USA as part of the FMS agreements (including two J-8II prototypes).[8] According to Chinese military sources who were involved in the Peace Pearl Program, these prototypes were returned 'as is', without the avionics upgrade kits.

In December 1992, after reports that China had transferred M-11 missile technology to Pakistan, the Bush Administration suspended the export of a Cray supercomputer which was to be used for meteorological purposes but which could be used for military applications. However, in January 1993, in one of the Bush Administration's last acts, the US Government approved the export of the computer, pending necessary licence processing. In August the Clinton Administration, citing further evidence that China had transferred M-11 missile technology to Pakistan, imposed sanctions on the two countries, banning US companies for two years from exporting items related to rockets and satellites to China or Pakistan and including a ban on dealing with 10 Chinese aerospace companies.

[7] Gertz, B., 'Chinese not likely to be crippled by U.S. arms cutoff', *Washington Times*, 6 June 1989, p. 11.

[8] 'Presidential decision on military sales to China', *US Department of State Dispatch*, 4 Jan. 1993, p. 10.

In mid- to late 1993 the Clinton Administration launched a series of high-level discussions with China. These included talks with senior Chinese military leaders during a visit to Beijing by Assistant Secretary of Defense for Regional Security Affairs Charles Freeman, the highest-level military contact between the two countries in nearly four years. The Clinton *rapprochement* with China was based on the assumption that through engagement China might be more forthcoming with regard to its future intentions.[9] While sanctions imposed in 1989 and 1993 which restricted the transfer of arms and other technology to China remained in place, there appeared to be an increased willingness on the part of the US Administration to loosen the interpretation of these restrictions. For example, the Clinton Administration reviewed the sanctions that were imposed in August 1993 in protest against the Chinese transfer of M-11 missile components to Pakistan and, in return for non-proliferation talks with China, decided in January 1994 to allow the export of three US-made satellites for launching by Chinese rockets (see below).

Since 1993, a number of specific agreements have been made between China and the USA involving items with potential military uses. For example, the Enstrom Helicopter Corporation reached an agreement in 1993 with Hubei Province authorities to co-produce light helicopters in China. Enstrom is a manufacturer of light helicopters which have civilian, police and military applications.[10] In November 1993 the Clinton Administration gave the final go-ahead for the transfer of the Cray supercomputer initially approved by President Bush earlier in the year. The computer was to be sent under strict monitoring conditions but is capable of performing calculations which would help China in developing its nuclear and ballistic missile capabilities.[11]

In early 1994 the Clinton Administration also took steps to allow the export of US commercial satellites to be launched by Chinese carrier rockets. The satellites to which this decision applies are for communications and television broadcasting purposes, but some critics of the policy argue that the Chinese military establishment will

[9] Barnard, R. C. and Opall, B., 'U.S. prods military dialogue with China', *Defense News*, 14–20 Mar. 1994, p. 1; and Sun, L. H., 'Military links resume after 4-year freeze', *International Herald Tribune*, 3 Nov. 1993, p. 2.

[10] 'China', *Asia–Pacific Defence Reporter*, Oct.–Nov. 1993, p. 20; and *Jane's All the World's Aircraft, 1993–94* (Jane's Information Group: Coulsdon, Surrey, 1993), p. 473.

[11] Sciolino, E., 'US to allow sale of supercomputer in gesture to China', *International Herald Tribune*, 21 Nov. 1993, p. 5.

ultimately benefit from the foreign-exchange revenues generated by their launch services and that it may benefit from US validation and integration analysis of Chinese satellite kick motors and upper-stage control systems.[12] The analyses test the reliability of Chinese rockets to place satellite payloads successfully in space. According to one report, the US Department of Commerce wishes to provide China with the technology necessary to make its own analyses, particularly in load analysis, which is critical for development of more advanced rocket systems, ballistic missiles and multiple independently targetable re-entry vehicle (MIRV) capabilities.[13] Reports in late 1994 indicated that the Clinton Administration considered an expansion of Sino-US cooperation in the field of space technology.[14]

In 1994 the Clinton Administration allowed the sale of AlliedSignal Garrett gas turbines to China to go forward, and as of early 1995 some 33 engines had been transferred. These engines were intended to power the K-8 training aircraft which China is developing jointly with Pakistan. In 1995 AlliedSignal declared its desire to sell the manufacturing technology for the engine to China as well. Critics of the proposed sale argued that such technology transfers would allow China to further develop its cruise missile capability. Others argue that the proposed future sales from Garrett to China will provide jobs in the USA, and that the transfer is not a proliferation concern in any case.

From 1993 to early 1995, there was a warming of relations between the two sides in the military sphere. The formal establishment of the Joint Commission on Defense Conversion took place during the visit of Secretary of Defense Perry in October 1994 as a means of bringing the two sides together on less sensitive military matters. This initiative was part of a broader effort to engage the Chinese military more closely, and, in the process, allow the two sides to avoid misunderstandings. During the course of 1993 and 1994, discussions as to possible military-use exports to China were held in defence policy circles in Washington.[15]

---

[12] Sokolski, H., 'Unseen dangers in China', *Armed Forces Journal International*, Feb. 1994, p. 25; and Sokolski, H., 'US satellites to China', *International Defense Review*, Apr. 1994, pp. 23–26. See also the comments of William C. Triplett in Richardson, M., 'Will US satellites help the military?', *Asia–Pacific Defence Reporter*, Feb.–Mar. 1994, p. 29.

[13] Sokolski, 'Unseen dangers in China' (note 12), p. 25.

[14] Lawler, A., 'U.S. eyes joint space efforts with Chinese', *Defense News*, 3–9 Oct. 1994, p. 1.

[15] For analysis and proposals on Sino-US military relations, see McNamara, R. S. *et al.*, *Sino-American Military Relations: Mutual Responsibilities in the Post-Cold War Era*

However, in spite of these developments, Sino-US relations have not come near the level of military-related cooperation the two countries experienced before 1989, particularly in the field of military technology transfer. As of 1995, US weapons and weapon technology transfers remained banned under the Presidential Directive issued in the wake of the Tiananmen Square massacre. Subsequent bans have been placed on military-related technologies and exchanges, such as the August 1993 decision by the Clinton Administration to restrict high-technology exports to certain entities in China believed to be related to the transfer of M-11 missiles and technology to Pakistan.

Appendix 3 summarizes the developments in Sino-US military technology cooperation since June 1989 and indicates the erratic character of relations in this area over the past five years. The bumpy ride for Sino-US military technology cooperation has put both sides on the defensive, which will make future cooperation in this area difficult although not impossible. Moreover, one of the principal motivations driving the USA to transfer arms and technology to China in the 1980s—the Soviet threat—has disappeared, making it all the more difficult to justify transfers of this nature. Most importantly, the shadow of the Tiananmen crackdown as well as the authoritarian character of the Chinese Government loom large in Washington and will inhibit military-related relationships and transfers between the United States and China.

Other Western suppliers

Regarding arms transfers, the European response to the Tiananmen Square crisis was less rigid than that of the USA. The British, French and Italian governments suspended arms sales to China but in some cases allowed for the continuation of programmes already in progress and, with the passage of time, inched back towards closer cooperation with China in this sphere. In June 1989 the Thatcher Government suspended future arms sales to China but allowed the continuation of the GEC-Marconi avionics upgrade programme for Chinese F-7M

(National Committee on US–China Relations: New York, Nov. 1994), especially pp. 19–23. See also Barnard, R. C. and Opall, B., 'U.S., China resume ties', *Defense News*, 11–17 July 1994, p. 1; and Barnard and Opall (note 9), p. 1. For a proposal to transfer defensive US military equipment to China, see Wilborn, T. L., *Security Cooperation with China: Analysis and a Proposal* (US Army War College, Strategic Studies Institute: Carlisle Barracks, Pa., 25 Nov. 1994), pp. 24–25.

fighters for which a new contract had been negotiated in March 1989; this programme is believed to have ended in 1990. In addition, there were reports in mid-1990 that China was negotiating with GEC to purchase 16 airborne early-warning (AEW) radars, systems which were developed as part of the British Nimrod project cancelled in 1986. The Nimrod systems could equip the Chinese Y-8 and Il-18 transport aircraft, reconfigured for an AEW role.[16] One report suggests that this programme was still under development in 1993 between GEC-Marconi and the Shaanxi Aircraft Company, producer of the Y-8.[17] The GEC-Ferranti Blue Hawk multi-mode pulse Doppler radar and the Marconi Defence Systems Apollo electronic warfare system were reportedly selected by China for installation on the Super-7 multi-role fighter under development in China, but thus far these aspirations have not been met.[18]

Even after the events around Tiananmen Square in June 1989, the French state-owned Aérospatiale company continued its joint-venture production of helicopters in China and made plans for further joint production agreements. The licensed production of 50 SA-365N Dauphin 2 (Chinese designation, Z-9A) helicopters for the PLA services continued without significant interruption, with the contract completed in 1992. The Harbin plant has since attempted to continue production of a Chinese version of this helicopter (Chinese designation, Z-9A-100) but with limited results. These Chinese military helicopters are powered by French Arriel 1C and 1C1 (Chinese designations, Z8 and WZ8A) turboshaft engines produced under licence. The helicopters produced with French assistance for use by the Chinese Navy will carry Thomson-CSF sensors and Crouzet magnetic anomaly detectors for ASW operations and are being stationed on Luda Class destroyers. It is expected that the helicopters will also equip other ships in the Chinese fleet such as the new Luhu Class destroyers. Chinese reports indicate that the Chinese-built version of the Z-9 is of the technological level of the French version.[19]

In another helicopter deal, China is a partner in a trilateral form of cooperation linking China (CATIC), Singapore (Singapore Aero-

[16] Barrie, D., 'Nimrod AEW radar for China', *Jane's Defence Weekly*, 16 June 1990, p. 1185.

[17] *Jane's All the World's Aircraft, 1993–94* (Jane's Information Group: Coulsdon, Surrey, 1993), p. 54.

[18] Dantes, E., 'An in-depth look at the Asia–Pacific air forces and future procurement', *Asian Defence Journal*, Jan. 1993, p. 22.

[19] *SWB: Far East*, FE/1598, 28 Jan. 1993, p. B2/4.

space) and a French-led consortium (Eurocopter) to co-develop and co-produce the EC-120 (formerly P-120L) light helicopter. Eurocopter will have a 61 per cent work-share (including the power train and final assembly), CATIC (through the Harbin Aircraft Manufacturing Corporation) will have a 24 per cent work-share (including the main fuselage, landing gear and fuel system), and Singapore Aerospace will have a 15 per cent work-share (including the doors and tail boom). The agreement includes on-site training of Chinese engineers at Aérospatiale facilities in France and the provision of French specialists to China. The helicopter, which can serve in a military role as an armed trainer and observation aircraft, is expected to make its first flight in 1995, with deliveries beginning in 1997.[20]

In October 1990 it was confirmed that the French company Thomson-CSF would sell China the two Crotale ship-to-air missile systems for use on Chinese Luda Class destroyers in a deal valued at $70 million. The deal included Crotale naval surface-to-air missiles, Sea Tiger search and target designation radars, and a tactical data handling system. At the time, the deal was said not to breach Western sanctions against China since the original agreement on the missile system dated back to 1986.[21] Also, reports in 1992 and 1993 indicated that the French-built DR-2000U missile targeting system has gone into the upgraded Han Class nuclear-powered submarines and that China was developing a new class of Ming submarines based on the French Agosta Class, possibly to include use of French weapons and sensors, but the extent of French cooperation on this programme, if any, is unclear.[22]

It has been confirmed that at least one of the new Jianghu II missile frigates recently produced in China will be equipped with Italian ILAS 324-mm triple ASW torpedo launchers and torpedoes, although this equipment was part of a shipment of launchers and torpedoes to China in the 1980s. In addition, these missile frigates are believed to be armed with a Breda 37-mm anti-aircraft gun, which is a significant

[20] Lambert, M. (ed.), *Jane's All the World's Aircraft, 1994–95* (Jane's Information Group: Coulsdon, Surrey, 1994), pp. 172–73; and Covault, C. and Sparaco, P., 'Europeans vie for sales in growth market', *Aviation Week & Space Technology*, 21 Feb. 1994, p. 78.

[21] 'French arms sales for the quarter', *Damocles in Brief*, summer 1993, p. 1; 'Paris moves to sell arms to Beijing', *International Herald Tribune*, 13–14 Oct. 1990, p. 3; and Hooton, T., 'French to upgrade Chinese Luda destroyers', *International Defense Review*, Aug. 1990, p. 920.

[22] Slade, S. L., 'New variant of Chinese SSNs revealed', *World Aerospace & Defense Intelligence*, 8 Oct. 1993, p. 17; and 'China', *World Weapons Review*, 9 Dec. 1992, p. 9.

provement over Chinese naval anti-aircraft systems and was also provided to China before June 1989.[23] The avionics upgrade programme of the Chinese A-5M fighter/ground attack aircraft resulted in the production of at least two prototypes which appeared publicly in 1991. The 24 A-5M aircraft delivered by China to Myanmar in 1994 probably included this upgrade package.

During the visit of German Chancellor Helmut Kohl to China in November 1993 (which generated some $3 billion worth of civil contracts for German firms), he noted that Germany had no problem transferring technology to China.[24] Deutsche Aerospace and China Aerospace Corporation—which have worked together in the past in the development of Chinese spacecraft—signed a joint venture agreement in 1994 which is expected to lead to the development of 20 new communications and earth survey spacecraft for China.[25] In addition, Chinese armoured vehicles have continued to be powered by German engines produced under licence; the new Luhu Class destroyers will have two German MTU diesel engines as part of their power plant.

Other smaller Western suppliers have also stepped up contacts with China. A report in March 1994 noted that Venga Aerospace Systems—a Canadian firm—would form a joint-venture corporation with the Baoshan Iron and Steel Company which envisages providing manufacturing facilities in China to build the Brushfire TG-10 jet aircraft and other aerospace components. The aircraft is expected to be produced in a two-seat trainer version and could be developed as a single-seat light attack aircraft.[26] Canadian sources also reported in mid-1994 that Canada was considering the transfer of the Challenger VIP jet transport aircraft to China. The deal, said to be worth $200 million, would include air reconnaissance equipment made in Israel.[27] In early 1995, defence analysts reported that the Spanish shipbuilding firm Bazan offered two designs to China for small aircraft-carriers

[23] On Italian contributions to China's Jianghu Class missile frigates, see Jacobs, G., 'PLAN's ASW frigate Siping', *Navy International*, Mar.–Apr. 1993, p. 69.

[24] 'China links', *The Independent*, 16 Nov. 1993, p. 10.

[25] Covault, C., 'Space programs surge in Asia/Pacific region', *Aviation Week & Space Technology*, 21 Feb. 1994, p. 73.

[26] 'Chinese venture revives Brushfire', *Jane's Defence Weekly*, 19 Mar. 1994, p. 25; 'The biennial aerospace business at Changi', *Asian Defence Journal*, Mar. 1994, p. 62; and *Jane's All the World's Aircraft, 1989–90* (Jane's Information Group: Coulsdon, Surrey, 1989), p. 30.

[27] 'Canada weighs plan to sell surveillance planes to Beijing', *International Herald Tribune*, 12 July 1994, p. 3.

that could accommodate aircraft such as the MiG-29K, the Dassault Rafale M, the McDonnell Douglas F/A-18 or the A-4M Skyhawk. While the cost of the vessel would be relatively low, China will need to continue developing doctrine and operational capacities to sustain an aircraft-carrier group before seriously moving forward on such a purchase.[28]

III. Acquisitions from Israel

Recent years have been marked by increasing Sino-Israeli cooperation on military and security matters. Past reports have included allegations of a wide range of military production cooperation: assistance for the guidance systems on CSS-2 ballistic missiles (which were sold to Saudi Arabia) and on the M-9 ballistic missile; technology to upgrade Chinese combat aircraft; and assistance in improving Chinese tanks. While it is extremely difficult to confirm such reports, it appears likely that Israel has offered significant technology cooperation to China, especially in the areas of aircraft and missile technology but also in tank weaponry technology.

The earliest reported military-related contacts between the two sides came in the mid-1970s.[29] Reports suggest that in the early to mid-1980s the Israeli Export Institute, SIBAT (the Foreign Defence Assistance and Defence Export department of the Israeli Ministry of Defence), Israeli Aircraft Industries and Israeli Military Industries signed agreements with counterparts in China to set up collaborative ventures on defence production. These agreements—valued in 1984 at $3 billion—included collaboration in the upgrading of Chinese tanks with new main guns and fire-control systems, assistance in the development of Chinese aircraft and missiles, and the provision of Israeli technical advisers (including the 1990 opening in China of an office of the Israeli Academy of Sciences).[30]

---

[28] Lok, J. J. and Karniol, R., 'Spain offers carrier designs to Chinese', *Jane's Defence Weekly*, 18 Feb. 1995, p. 8.

[29] The following section describing the background to Sino-Israeli defence cooperation is drawn from Kumaraswamy, P. R., 'The star and the dragon: an overview of Israeli–PRC military relations', *Issues & Studies*, Apr. 1994, pp. 36–55.

[30] 'United States', *Asia–Pacific Defence Reporter*, Sep. 1990, p. 30; 'US rift over secret Chinese–Israeli deals', *Jane's Defence Weekly*, 15 Dec. 1984, p. 1051; and 'London Times: Israel to modernize 9,000 Chinese battle tanks', *International Defense DMS Intelligence*, 29 Oct. 1984, p. 1.

While most of the military cooperation was conducted in secret, the formal establishment of diplomatic relations between China and Israel in 1992 has resulted in an active and open exchange of scientific, military and industrial delegations. Even before the establishment of diplomatic ties, secret meetings often came into the open. For example, in 1988 the Israeli consul in Hong Kong led a delegation to China to demonstrate military equipment to the PLA. The visit was revealed when a member of the delegation was caught by Hong Kong authorities travelling with a false passport as he left China. Israeli Defence Minister Moshe Arens travelled to China in 1991, and his visit was subsequently reported in the international press. Whether official or otherwise, the long-term effort by China and Israel to develop closer military cooperation has contributed to the transfer of weapon technology from Israel to China.

The October 1993 visit to China by Israeli Prime Minister Yitzhak Rabin, the Director-General of the Israeli Defence Ministry, David Ivri, and other defence officials further fuelled suspicions of defence-related collaboration between China and Israel. On the issue of Sino-Israeli cooperation on military technology, Ivri said, 'There are security relations. It certainly can be said that there is such a thing—no doubt', but he would not specify the extent of those ties.[31] Rabin's visit coincided with the release by the US Senate Governmental Affairs Committee of a report which included written testimony by CIA chief R. James Woolsey on Sino-Israeli military collaboration. Woolsey noted: 'Building on a long history of close defense industrial relations—including work on China's next generation fighter, air-to-air missiles, and tank programs—and the establishment of diplomatic relations in January 1992, China and Israel appear to be moving toward formalizing and broadening their military technical co-operation'. He added: 'Beijing probably hopes to tap Israeli expertise for cooperative development of military technologies, such as advanced tank power plants and airborne radar systems, that the Chinese would have difficulty producing on their own'.[32]

Specifically, the Senate report alleged that Israel sold to China technology related to the US-financed Lavi fighter programme (which was cancelled in 1987), Sidewinder air-to-air missile technology (in

---

[31] Quoted in 'Rabin strengthens ties, signs aviation pact with China', *Jerusalem Post International Edition*, 23 Oct. 1994, p. 24.

[32] Woolsey quoted in Gordon, M. R., 'Israel sold weapons to China', *International Herald Tribune*, 13 Oct. 1993, p. 5.

the form of the Israeli Python III air-to-air missile) and information related to the AIM-7 Sparrow air-to-air missile. The report added that Israel had re-exported technology not only from the United States but also from other Western sources, including France, Germany and the United Kingdom.[33] According to an unofficial account, Israeli transfers of technology to China can be valued at $2–3 billion.[34]

Close Sino-Israeli cooperation is likely to continue. Chinese Vice-Premier Zou Jiahua, whose professional background and current portfolio includes a strong interest in Chinese defence industries, visited Israel in October 1994 and made trips to defence firms on his itinerary. While in Israel, Zou met with the country's prime minister and defence minister, as well as two leading persons responsible for establishing Sino-Israeli miltary ties—former Defence Minister Moshe Arens and Shoul Eisenberg, an Israeli businessman.[35]

Missile technology

In the area of missile technology, Israel has allegedly supplied assistance to China in air defence and air-to-air missiles. In early 1993, a report based on Pentagon sources claimed that Israel had transferred anti-tactical ballistic missile (ATBM) technology (based on the US Patriot missile) to China in return for information on the Chinese M series ballistic missiles. It was not clear from the reports whether the transfer took place with the knowledge of the Israeli Government or if it was part of a 'rogue' operation. US officials did not deny that China had received Patriot technology, but open sources do not state with certainty exactly what form of transfer—hardware, software and/or documents—took place. An inter-agency review team led by the Department of State concluded in 1992 that no evidence existed to support the claim that the Patriot technology in China had come from Israel.[36]

---

[33] See Hunter, J., 'Military collaboration', *Middle East International*, 22 Oct. 1993, pp. 8–9; 'Israelis selling advanced weapons technology to China', *World Aerospace & Defense Intelligence*, 22 Oct. 1993, p. 20; and 'Report tells of Israel–PRC technology deal', *World Aerospace & Defense Intelligence*, 15 Oct. 1993, p. 15.

[34] Cockburn, P. 'Israel accused of selling US secrets to China', *The Independent*, 13 Oct. 1993, p. 13. This article quotes a former State Department analyst, Morton Miller, who values Israeli technology transfers to China as between $8 billion and $10 billion.

[35] See 'Chinese confer with Israeli defense firms', *Defense News*, 10–16 Oct. 1994, p. 2; and 'Vice-Premier in Israel', *Far Eastern Economic Review*, 13 Oct. 1994, p. 13.

[36] On the transfer of Patriot missile technology to China, see Fulghum, D. A., 'Defense Dept. confirms Patriot technology diverted', *Aviation Week & Space Technology*, 1 Feb.

Israeli Python III air-to-air missile technology appears to be included in production of the Chinese PL-9 AAMs which arm Chinese fighters. Technology from the Python III may also be present in the PL-8H naval defence surface-to-air missiles, unveiled in 1991, and currently in service with the PLA Navy.

Avionics and aircraft

Some reports allege that Israel is assisting China in such areas as electronic warfare (EW), electronic intelligence (ELINT), airborne early-warning (AEW) and avionics technologies for Chinese combat aircraft that are drawn from the Lavi fighter programme.[37] Of these programmes, perhaps most important is the conversion of Chinese Y-8 transport aircraft to AEW capabilities, transferring technologies and hardware related to Israel's Phalcon AEW system.[38] However, these reports are not confirmed and such systems have not been reported to be in operation.

Much attention has been focused on the alleged provision of advanced jet fighter technology to China from Israel. This programme reportedly draws heavily on technologies developed as part of the US–Israeli Lavi project, which was cancelled in 1987. Reports appearing at the end of 1994 and in early 1995 indicated that Sino-Israeli cooperation on this programme had made significant advances. A prototype of the new jet, dubbed the J-10 and developed jointly by the Chengdu Aircraft Corporation and Israeli Aircraft Industries, was reportedly near completion and was scheduled to make test flights in 1996. In particular, Israel is believed to have provided assistance in the aircraft's avionics suite, including a head-up display and radar-guided missile capability, all of which are considerably more advanced than the systems China had previously. Defence analysts suggest that the avionics suite may also be drawn from the Israeli Air-

---

1993, p. 26; and Fulghum, D. A., 'China exploiting U.S. Patriot secrets', *Aviation Week & Space Technology*, 18 Jan. 1993, p. 20.

[37] Details of these systems can be found in Sengupta, P., 'China expands air forces', *Military Technology*, Aug. 1992, p. 50.

[38] Sengupta (note 37), p. 50; and Jacobs, K., 'China's military modernization and the South China Sea', *Jane's Intelligence Review*, June 1992, p. 281. The Phalcon AEW system is described in *Jane's Radar and Electronic Warfare Systems, 1992–93* (Jane's Information Group: Coulsdon, Surrey, 1992), p. 221.

craft Industries F-5 avionics upgrade programme, which itself was developed from the Lavi programme.[39]

Israel does not deny that there has been a transfer of aircraft technology to China. David Ivri, Director-General of the Israeli Defence Ministry, said that Israel was offering China 'some technology on aircraft' but that the amount was very small. He denied that US technology was included in the transfer, noting that the Lavi technology was already quite old and that subsequent developments to this know-how had been made by Israel.[40]

Other programmes

In addition to assistance in missiles and aircraft, Israel is believed to have helped China in the development of tank weapon technology. This assistance includes upgrading of Chinese tanks with new main guns and fire-control systems. Israeli radar technology is reportedly installed on upgraded Han Class nuclear submarines: the Timnex 4CH(V)2 electronic surveillance measure (ESM) system, which is designed for submarine-launched anti-ship missiles, appears to be part of the targeting system for the submarines. If installed, this system would give the Chinese an over-the-horizon targeting capability which they formerly did not have.[41]

Russian and Israeli arms exports to China share similarities. The Israeli arms industries have been well developed over the years and are now under pressure to export in order to save jobs and technological expertise. Moreover, China recognizes the benefits it can gain from the high-level technology that may be available from Israel. Also, as in the case of Sino-Russian contacts, Israel hopes to sell hardware and off-the-shelf systems, while China is mainly interested in receiving technology and production expertise. These differences may slow the rapid development of Sino-Israeli ties in this sphere, but

[39] On the Sino-Israeli development of a new-generation fighter, see Fulghum, D. A., 'New Chinese fighter nears prototyping', *Aviation Week & Space Technology*, 13 Mar. 1995, pp. 26–27; Mann, J., 'Israeli sale of arms technology to China irks U.S.', *International Herald Tribune*, 29 Dec. 1994, p. 1; Barrie, D., 'Chinese tonic', *Flight International*, 9–15 Nov. 1994, p. 16; and 'Israel co-operates with China on secret fighter', *Flight International*, 2–8 Nov. 1994, p. 4.

[40] 'Israel tries to clear up jet dispute', *International Herald Tribune*, 4 Jan. 1995, p. 2.

[41] Slade, S. L., 'New variant of Chinese SSNs revealed', *World Aerospace & Defense Intelligence*, 8 Oct. 1993, p. 17.

it does seem that their relationship will be sustained in the years ahead.

Reports on Sino-Israeli military technology cooperation must be treated with proper caution, however. While speculation abounds, evidence as to the nature, scope and type of cooperation on most programmes remains sketchy and difficult to interpret with certainty.

IV. Other sources of supply

Pakistan and Iran

Pakistan has been one of China's closest allies for nearly 30 years and a major recipient of Chinese weapons and military technology; it has also served as a supplier of weapons and military technology to China. China and Pakistan work closely and share information and technology on a number of military production projects, including the development and manufacture of the Pakistani MBT and the K-8 jet trainer, development of Pakistani missile systems and development of the FC-1 fighter aircraft.[42] Reports in 1992 and 1993 suggested that Pakistan transferred Stinger man-portable anti-aircraft missiles which in the mid-1980s were exported in large numbers to the Afghan Mujahideen via the Pakistani Inter-Services Intelligence Agency.[43] It is difficult to know with certainty how much the relationship is two-way—perhaps most of the technology and hardware flow goes from China to Pakistan. However, it is probably a safe assumption that Pakistan is willing to share what it can with its Chinese patron.

It is also difficult to know the exact extent and nature of Sino-Iranian ties in this type of cooperation. China is believed to be working with Iran on the development of ballistic missiles such as the M-7 (Project 8610) 180-km range missile, the M-9 600-km missile and the M-18 1000-km missile.[44] It is unclear, however, how much assistance

---

[42] 'China, Pakistan to develop new aircraft', *Times of India*, 6 June 1995, p. 15; and Bickers, C., 'Sino-Pakistan fighter set to fly by 1997', *Jane's Defence Weekly*, 17 June 1995, p. 3.

[43] 'Sting in the tail', *Far Eastern Economic Review*, 28 Oct. 1993, p. 9; and 'Stingers go to China', *Asian Recorder*, 10–16 June 1992, p. 22363.

[44] Opall, B., 'US queries China on Iran', *Defense News*, 19–25 June 1995, p. 1; 'China sending Iran arms parts, US finds', *New York Times*, 22 June 1995, p. 1; and Reed, J., *Defence Exports: Current Concerns* (Jane's Information Group: Coulsdon, Surrey, Apr. 1993), pp. 4–5.

Iran provides to China in these programmes. It is more clear that Ir\
served as the provider of technologies in at least two other cases.

1. Iran is believed to have provided China with Soviet equipment
and technology, especially aircraft and aircraft technology, which
came into Iranian hands as a result of the 1980–88 Iraq–Iran War and
when Iraqi pilots defected to Iran with Soviet-made aircraft during the
1991 Persian Gulf War. These transfers may have included the Su-22,
the Su-24, the Su-25 and the MiG-29. In exchange, China provided
Iran with tanks, artillery and other weapons.[45] A Japanese wire service
reported in 1993 that Iran was providing China with an undisclosed
number of MiG-29s to assist in upgrading the Chinese F-7 in return
for missile technology and a nuclear power station.[46]

2. Iran assisted China in the development of in-flight refuelling
technology, probably by providing US aerial refuelling systems in
Iranian possession, including Beech refuelling pods and bolt-on
probes originally provided to the Iranian Government under the
Shah.[47]

Sources of dual-use technology

In addition to cooperation which clearly involves items for military
use, a wide range of activities were undertaken by China and foreign
partners in producing items under licence or as subcontractors which
may contribute to improving Chinese military and technological
capabilities. While the grey area of 'dual-use' technologies and production is beyond the scope of this report, it is interesting to note the
extent of Chinese cooperation with foreign partners across a number
of industrial sectors but especially in the area of aerospace, in the production of system components (see table 4.1). Experience in the
development and production of these components may assist China by
introducing advanced equipment and techniques and by providing
greater expertise in Western technologies.

It remains unclear just how much business the Chinese aerospace
industry will be able to generate with foreign partners, and its future

[45] 'PRC to buy Flankers, eyes Iraqi aircraft', *International Defense Review*, May 1991,
p. 389.
[46] *SWB: Far East*, FE/1585, 13 Jan. 1993, p. A1/2.
[47] See Sengupta (note 37), p. 50; *World Weapons Review*, 10 Apr. 1991, p. 16; and
'Fuelling speculation', *Far Eastern Economic Review*, 20 Feb. 1991, p. 9.

Table 4.1. Principal Chinese agreements with foreign firms in the aircraft sector, 1990–95

Chinese partner	Foreign partner(s)	Description
AVIC	McDonnell Douglas	Assembly of MD-82, MD-82T and MD-90 transport aircraft
AVIC	Daewoo Heavy Industries	Memorandum of Understanding signed in Oct. 1993 to manufacture 100-seat regional transport aircraft
AVIC	Samsung Daimler-Benz Aerospace	Three-way agreement reached in 1995 with plans to build 120-seat aircraft
CAC	McDonnell Douglas	Nose cones for MD-80 series aircraft, both for assembly programme in China and for aircraft produced in the USA
CAREC	General Electric	Turbine discs
CAREC	General Electric	Co-development of WJ5E engine for Y-7-200B transport aircraft
CAREC	Rolls-Royce	Turbine blades and vanes
CATIC	Eurocopter/Singapore Aerospace	Cooperation on design and development, production of main composite/alloy fuselage, fuel and hydraulic systems for EC-120 helicopter
CNAEC	Collins	Licensed production of flight instrumentation systems
HAMC	British Aerospace	Cargo and landing gear doors for BAe 146 transport aircraft
HAMC	Sikorsky	Machined parts for the UH-60 Blackhawk helicopter
HAMC	Shorts Brothers	Wing boxes and cabin doors for Shorts 360 aircraft
Hubei Province	Enstrom Helicopter	Agreement to co-produce light helicopter
LETI	Collins	Production of receiver–transmitter for WXR-700 radar systems
SAC	Airbus Industrie	Wing ribs and emergency hatches for Airbus 320 aircraft

Chinese partner	Foreign partner(s)	Description
SAC	de Havilland	Cargo doors for de Havilland Dash 8 aircraft
SAC	Lockheed	Tail cone, landing gear door, pylon components for C-130 Hercules transport aircraft
XAC	Airbus Industrie	Access doors for A300 aircraft
XAC	Aerospatiale/Alenia	Wing boxes and access doors for ATR42 transport aircraft
XAC	Boeing	Developing wing design for Y-7-200B transport aircraft
XAC	Boeing	Vertical fins and forward access doors for Boeing 737 aircraft
XAC	Canadair	Water-bomber pylons, water tanks and doors for CL215 aircraft

Acronyms: AVIC = Aviation Industries of China; CAC = Chengdu Aircraft Industrial Corporation; CAREC = China National Aeroengine Corporation; CATIC = China National Aerotechnology Import–Export Corporation; CNAEC = China National Airborne Equipment Corporation; HAMC = Harbin Aircraft Manufacturing Corporation; LETI = Leihua Electronics Technology Institute; SAC = Shenyang Aircraft Corporation; XAC = Xian Aircraft Corporation.

Sources: Jane's All the World's Aircraft (Jane's Information Group: Coulsdon, Surrey, several editions). See also Lindemann, M., 'Dasa and Samsung plan to develop aircraft with China', *Financial Times*, 7 Mar. 1995, p. 16.

as a competitive producer of either military or civil aircraft is open to question. *Jane's* notes, for example, that 'China may in fact be less of a threat to the stability of the Western aircraft market than South Korea, Taiwan, Indonesia, and similar countries', suggesting that expanded and widespread international collaboration between China and Western aerospace manufacturers (and related spin-offs to military use) may not materialize.[48] So far, most cooperative arrangements

---

[48] *Jane's All the World's Aircraft, 1993–94* (Jane's Information Group: Coulsdon, Surrey, 1993), p. [17]; see also the analysis of China's aeronautics industry in United States General Accounting Office, *Asian Aeronautics: Technology Acquisition Drives Industry Development* (US General Accounting Office: Washington, DC, 4 May 1994).

between China and foreign aerospace firms involve the production of relatively simple aircraft parts and are relatively small contracts. For example, Xian Aircraft Corporation earned approximately $12 million in 1992 manufacturing subcontracted parts for foreign aerospace companies, and the Harbin Aircraft Manufacturing Corporation earned $3.2 million in 1992 producing parts for foreign companies. However, both of these facilities can significantly enlarge their production capacity to supply foreign partners.[49]

In the early 1990s, China made efforts to purchase some $2 billion worth of US computer chip manufacturing equipment. The capability to produce computer chips is fundamental to China's economic modernization programme, with applications ranging from use in telecommunications, computers and electronics to use in rockets, satellites and weapons.[50] However, the US semiconductor industry appeared cautious about the prospects of business with China, citing problems of profit repatriation, slow start-up periods and problems related to intellectual property rights.[51]

In any event, according to several Western and Chinese researchers, the nature and organization of Chinese military R&D and production tend to obstruct the transfer of dual-use technologies from the civilian sector.[52] The cross-over of technology from the civilian side to the military side will probably be a difficult manœuvre in the Chinese case.

V. Conclusions

This review of contemporary military-related imports by China from sources other than Russia points to several implications about Chinese arms acquisitions, both for the contemporary period and for the future. It appears that with the exception perhaps of imports from Israel, which are difficult to identify from the open literature, Chinese

[49] Proctor, P., 'Harbin uses new helicopter program to advance global manufacturing role', *Aviation Week & Space Technology*, 3 Feb. 1992, p. 48; and Proctor, P., 'China's Xian Aircraft Corp. emphasizes Y-7 production, foreign subcontracts', *Aviation Week & Space Technology*, 24 Feb. 1992, p. 112.

[50] Southerland, D., 'China seeks chips made in U.S.A.', *International Herald Tribune*, 19 Nov. 1992, p. 1.

[51] Southerland (note 50), p. 1.

[52] Arnett, E., 'Military technology: the case of China', in *SIPRI Yearbook 1995: Armaments, Disarmament and International Security* (Oxford University Press: Oxford, 1995), p. 369.

arms acquisitions from these non-Russian sources have tended to be relatively sparse and problematic. Taken collectively, these transfers do not appear to provide China with the means to improve its military technology and arms production capacity significantly or to make swift comprehensive improvements in the capabilities of the PLA.

In certain limited areas, however, such as in developing improved air and naval surveillance and aerial refuelling, China may experience relatively rapid advances. The question remains as to the future nature and extent of cooperation with non-Russian suppliers, especially those in the West, as memories of the Tiananmen Square massacre fade. While China presents a potentially lucrative market for suppliers faced with declining procurement orders, it is difficult to foresee a rush in arms sales to China. Policies in China as well as in the West will tend to weigh against this. Rather, developments in China's military capability derived from Western weapons and military technology will for the most part continue to move ahead slowly and erratically.

While these developments can be traced in part to the sanctions placed on China by major suppliers in 1989, they are more deeply a reflection of at least three constant currents in Chinese foreign arms acquisitions policies: preference for technology and know-how over off-the-shelf acquisitions; fear of dependence on foreign suppliers; and unhappy memories of previous arms and arms technology acquisitions from Western suppliers. China remains committed to foreign supply arrangements which will involve transfers of technology and know-how rather than off-the-shelf purchases. Those major deals which can be cited between China and non-Russian suppliers have tended to be short-lived, typically reaching only the prototype stage and not going into production (see table 4.2).

Furthermore, China does not wish to become dependent on foreign suppliers and will continue to seek the means to produce advanced weapons indigenously. Even if ties between China and the West improve in the years ahead, China is likely to remain sceptical about close cooperation in military production or arms transfers owing to past arrangements which China views as less than beneficial. For example, Beijing remains sensitive over the failed Peace Pearl Program, in which China spent nearly $400 million only to receive incomplete avionics systems when the programme was terminated. China can be expected to weigh critically the pros and cons of any

Table 4.2. Military technology imports from non-Soviet/Russian sources for weapon systems produced in China, 1975–95

Weapon system	Partner(s)	Description
Aircraft		
A-5K attack aircraft	Thomson-CSF	In a deal signed in 1987, Thomson-CSF agreed to provide new navigation and attack system upgrade, including HUD, laser range-finder, inertial navigation system, radio altimeter, new instrumentation panel, video camera and electricity generation system; programme resulted in 2 prototypes which flew in 1988 and 1989; programme terminated in 1990
A-5M attack aircraft	Aeritalia/Alenia Litton	Aeritalia/Alenia provided all-weather navigation and attack system, electronic countermeasures system and HUD; Litton provided LN-39A inertial navigation system
B-7 attack aircraft	Rolls-Royce	The Rolls-Royce Spey Mk 202 engines reportedly powered initial prototypes of this aircraft
F-7M Airguard fighter	GEC-Marconi Collins	Avionics suite includes Type 956 HUDWAC, Collins Skyranger radar, AD3400 communication system; contracted beginning in 1989 to deliver *c.* 100 avionics and navigation kits for F-7MP, a modified version of the F-7M
J-8II fighter	IAI Grumman	Reported provision of Lavi EI/M-2034 fire-control radar; Peace Pearl Program contracted Grumman in 1987 to provide avionics kits, programme cancelled in 1990
K-8 jet trainer	PAC Bendix/King Collins AlliedSignal	PAC has 25% share in joint design and co-production project; Bendix/King provides tactical air navigation system; Collins provides EFIS-86 flight instrumentation system (licence-produced in China); AlliedSignal provided Garrett TFE731-2A-2A turbofan engine for initial production models; licensed production of Garrett engine is currently delayed

Weapon system	Partner(s)	Description
Super-7 fighter	Grumman GEC-Ferranti GEC-Marconi Alenia	CATIC and Grumman signed initial contract in Oct. 1988; Grumman's initial cooperation in redesign work and wind tunnel testing; recommended the GE404 engine; GEC-Ferranti Blue Hawk radar, Marconi Apollo electronic warfare pod and Alenia Aspide AAM were reported in early 1993 to be included in development of Super-7 fighter; China continues to seek foreign partners for this made-for-export upgrade programme of the F-7M fighter
Y-8 maritime patrol	IAI GEC-Marconi Litton Collins	Reported provision of AEW technology from Israeli Phalcon aircraft; GEC-Marconi assisting in development of AEW version of Y-8; export version of this aircraft, Y-8D, has main avionics systems from Litton and Collins; Litton and Collins provide avionics for Y-8X, maritime patrol version of this aircraft
Z-9A-100 helicopter	Aérospatiale Turbomeca Arriel Crouzet Thomson-CSF	Licensed production completed in 1992; now built under domestic contract including deliveries to PLA services; almost entirely local manufacture; PRC produces Arriel 1C and 1C1 (Chinese designation Z8 and WZ8A) turboshaft engines under licence for Z-9A-100 helicopter; carries Thomson-CSF sensors and Crouzet magnetic anomaly detector for ASW

Armour

T-59 main battle tank	MEL Marconi Radar	MEL supplied China with 30 sets of Royal Ordnance passive night vision equipment, including image-intensified periscopes for use by T-59 MBT commander, driver and gunner; Royal Ordnance provided 105-mm L7A3 rifled main gun in upgrade package on 4 test models shown in Pakistan in 1987;

Table 4.2 contd

Weapon system	Partner(s)	Description
		the 105-mm rifled gun (possibly Israeli) is now standard equipment on new-generation Chinese MBTs, including the T-79, T-80 and T-85; in 1985 Marconi Radar and Control Systems supplied China with a Marksman twin 35-mm air defence turret for installation on the T-59 MBT chassis
NFV-1 IFV	FMC	Jointly developed by NORINCO and FMC based on June 1986 agreement; FMC provided electric-drive turret weapon station armed with 25-mm McDonnell Douglas Helicopters M242 chain gun as main armament and 7.62-mm machine gun; development is complete for this system, but no serial production has commenced for NGV-1
IFV	Giat Deutz	Armoured personnel carrier first seen in 1988; a Chinese fighting vehicle (6 x 6) WZ 551 APC mounted with a Giat Drager powered 1-man turret armed with a 25-mm Giat Industries M811 main gun, a 7.62-mm machine-gun, and electronically controlled smoke dischargers; powered by Deutz V-8 diesel engine made under licence in China
NVH-1 IFV	Vickers Deutz	Based on a 1984 agreement between NORINCO and Vickers Defense systems provides 2-man, all-welded armoured steel turret with McDonnell Douglas Helicopters 25-mm M242 chain gun as main weapon and 7.62-mm machine-gun; powered by Deutz V-8 diesel engine made under licence in China; as of 1993, development complete but not in serial production
Naval vessels		
Hainan Class	Racal	Agreement signed in 1987 between British Racal and China State Ship-

Weapon system	Partner(s)	Description
		building Corporation giving Racal responsibility for the outfitting of weapons and electronic systems for Hainan class patrol boats; current status of the programme is uncertain, but appears to have been stalled
Jianghu Class Type II frigate	Thomson-CSF ILAS Racal	At least one vessel of this class has a Thomson-CSF Creusot Loire 100-mm naval gun, two of which were supplied to China in late 1980s; Italian ILAS provided in 1980s torpedo launchers for these vessels; Racal navigation radar is confirmed in use on at least one of the frigates in this class
Jiangwei Class frigate	Thomson-CSF	Thomson-CSF Crotale octuple surface-to-air missile launcher arms this new class of frigates, first commissioned in 1992
Luhu Class destroyer	Thomson-CSF General Electric MTU	Thomson-CSF Crotale octuple surface-to-air missile launcher arms this new class of destroyers; at least 1 of these vessels is powered by 2 General Electric LM2500 twin gas turbine engines; German MTU 12V 1163 TB83 diesel engines are part of propulsion system for this class of vessel

Acronyms: HUD = head-up display; HUDWAC = head-up display and weapon aiming computer; IAI = Israel Aircraft Industries; IFV = infantry fighting vehicle; MBT = main battle tank; MTU = Motoren und Turbinen Union; NORINCO = China North Industries Corporation; PAC = Pakistan Aeronautical Complex.

Sources: Jane's All the World's Aircraft (Jane's Information Group: Coulsdon, Surrey, several editions); *Jane's Fighting Ships* (Jane's Information Group: Coulsdon, Surrey, several editions); *Jane's Armour and Artillery* (Jane's Information Group: Coulsdon, Surrey, several editions); *Jane's Naval Weapons Systems* (Jane's Information Group: Coulsdon, Surrey, 1992); *Jane's Air-Launched Weapons* (Jane's Information Group: Coulsdon, Surrey, 1988); and SIPRI arms trade database, 1994.

future defence trade arrangements with the USA or other major Western suppliers.[53]

In addition, Western governments harbour suspicions about providing China with advanced weapons and technology. China has never been a major recipient of weapons and military technology from the West; those transfers which have taken place have typically been approved on a relatively limited and carefully reviewed basis, often after much political and economic soul-searching at home. Even as the memories of the Tiananmen Square tragedy become more distant, China remains a strategic question-mark for Western powers. Unilateral and multilateral controls—both reflections of the West's continued uneasiness about Chinese strategic intentions—will limit the extent of defence trade cooperation to dual-use items, defensive systems and technologies of limited sophistication. Indeed, China occupies a paradoxical position within some multilateral arms control regimes. On the one hand, the cooperation of China as an *exporter* is required to limit the proliferation of weapons and technologies; on the other hand, the West recognizes a need to limit China as an *importer* of weapons and technology.

Certain trends suggest that China's effort to acquire foreign arms will have some limited success. Pressures by arms manufacturers in the West to open the defence trade market in China will continue to be strong, and, in the coming years, increased levels of defence trade cooperation between China and the West can be expected. In the end, China can probably not rely on such trade, and will need to turn to such suppliers as Russia and Israel, as well as to its own indigenous resources, to further develop its weapons and military technology.

[53] Opall, B., 'Chinese encounter dilemma in U.S. trade', *Defense News*, 11–17 July 1994, p. 6.

5. Future arms acquisitions: influences and implications

When we stress self-reliance, we do not mean we will close the door to pursue our own construction. What we mean is to actively create the conditions to import advanced technology from abroad and borrow every useful experience. . . . One of the basic principles of modernisation of weapons and equipment in our Army is to mainly rely on our own strength for regeneration, while selectively importing advanced technology from abroad, centering on some areas. (General Liu Huaqing, Vice-Chairman of the Chinese Central Military Commission, 1993[1])

I. Introduction

In this chapter, four key issues are addressed regarding the future influences on and implications of Chinese arms imports: (*a*) domestic developments which are likely to shape future weapon acquisition policy; (*b*) international developments which are likely to shape future weapon acquisition policy; (*c*) the arms procurement choices that may be taken in response to these developments; and (*d*) the implications of these choices for regional security.

In reviewing these four issues, several conclusions are drawn about the future direction and impact of Chinese arms acquisitions from abroad. China will continue to face a multitude of difficult obstacles and choices as it strives to improve its military standing in part through the import of weapon systems and technologies. Given these problems, there are limits to how much China can reasonably expect to achieve over the next 10–15 years. At the same time, China's domestic and international environments are likely to foster continued and increased efforts by Beijing to modernize its forces with the help of weapon and technology imports. In addition, and perhaps more important than China's growth as a military power, China's burgeoning economic and political influence in the region is likely to continue, whether or not its military power can keep pace. It will be this challenge—seeking to possess military strength commensurate with

---

[1] Quoted from *Jiefangjun Bao* [Liberation army daily], 6 Aug. 1993, p. 1, and translated in 'Liu Huaqing writes on modernization', Foreign Broadcast Information Service, *Daily Report–China* (hereafter FBIS-CHI), 18 Aug. 1993, p. 19.

its increasing regional and international presence and suited to its self-perception of being a great power—that will engage Chinese military planners in the years ahead.

II. The domestic environment

Influence of economic factors

Two important economic factors which affect Chinese arms imports stand out for consideration. The first concerns the economic resources available to the Chinese military establishment to pursue military imports; the second concerns the impact of economic development and reform on China's indigenous arms-development and -production capacity.

While the resources available to the Chinese military may be on the rise, there remain questions as to the effect these increases have on China's ability to modernize its forces through imports of weapons and technologies. One school of thought argues that the Chinese military is too hard pressed by inflation and the increasing costs of personnel and maintenance to devote substantial resources to the purchase of weapons from abroad. This school makes the further point that, even when considering the unofficial calculations of actual Chinese defence expenditure in recent years, growth in Chinese military spending has remained sluggish and has even declined in some years, allowing for inflation and currency devaluation. According to the US Arms Control and Disarmament Agency (ACDA), in the period 1983–93 Chinese military spending steadily declined as a percentage of both GNP and central government expenditure (CGE) and showed little significant real increase over the same period, remaining at $50–$56 billion a year[2] (see table 5.1). The devaluation of the Chinese renminbi in 1994 further supports the argument that financial constraints will inhibit Chinese military modernizers from making significant purchases from abroad.

While not necessarily disagreeing with this analysis, another school of thought points out that military technologies from abroad can be acquired in more ways than only the traditional means of direct purchase and may involve barter trade, hiring of foreign expertise and

[2] US Arms Control and Disarmament Agency, *World Military Expenditures and Arms Transfers, 1993–1994* (US Government Printing Office: Washington, DC, Feb. 1995), p. 58.

Table 5.1. Chinese military expenditure, 1983–93

Figures are in constant (1993) US$ m., and as a share of gross national product (GNP) and central government expenditure (CGE).

Year	Annual spending	% of GNP	% of CGE
1983	53 050	6.8	30.4
1984	52 140	5.8	26.1
1985	52 160	5.1	23.8
1986	50 960	4.6	19.3
1987	51 400	4.2	19.5
1988	52 040	3.8	20.0
1989	51 320	3.6	19.1
1990	54 110	3.7	18.8
1991	52 000	3.3	17.3
1992	54 870	3.0	16.9
1993	56 170	2.7	16.2

Source: US Arms Control and Disarmament Agency, *World Military Expenditures and Arms Transfers, 1993–1994* (US Government Printing Office: Washington, DC, Feb. 1995), p. 58. The source notes that these are 'rough estimates'.

sharing of intelligence and technologies, all of which methods China has employed over the past 20 years to import weapons and military technology. Furthermore, the estimates of total Chinese military expenditure do not disaggregate figures for arms imports or military R&D, which may be on the rise, even as total spending remains relatively steady. Observers make the point that Chinese spending on R&D is receiving new emphasis, with one report claiming that 'half the increase in total defence spending' may be going towards military R&D.[3] It should also be noted that, in spite of Chinese rhetoric on the poverty of its military establishment, perhaps some $2–3 billion has been spent on arms procurement from Russia in recent years, with further commitments perhaps amounting to an additional $1.5–2 billion in the future. In addition, an estimated $2–3 billion worth of purchases from Israel since the early 1980s should also be included. SIPRI estimates that the volume of Chinese arms imports showed a considerable increase for 1992, largely owing to the Su-27 purchase, but a sharp decline for 1993–94 (see table 5.2).

[3] 'China's new model army', *The Economist*, 11 June 1994, p. 55. See also the comments of John Frankenstein in Mecham, M., 'China's military budget up 20%; U.S. to aid industry', *Aviation Week & Space Technology*, 21 Mar. 1994, p. 62.

Table 5.2. Volume of Chinese arms imports, 1990–94

Figures are in SIPRI trend-indicator values, expressed in constant 1990 US$ m. The 1990–94 total differs due to rounding.

1990	1991	1992	1993	1994	**1990–94**
125	151	1 976	679	2	**2 932**

Source: Anthony, I., *et al.*, 'The trade in major conventional weapons', *SIPRI Yearbook 1995: Armaments, Disarmament and International Security* (Oxford University Press: Oxford, 1995), table 14.2, pp. 494–95.

Taken together, these two indicators of China's economic wherewithal to purchase foreign weapons suggest that, while there appears to be a willingness to spend on some items, this tendency is not as yet indicative of a massive effort to upgrade the Chinese military through shopping sprees abroad. While there is some evidence that China is devoting greater resources to science and technology and military R&D, spending in these sectors remains relatively modest. David Shambaugh estimates that a portion of the annual budget of approximately $5 billion of the State Science and Technology Commission goes to help support COSTIND military R&D projects, and other sources suggest that Chinese defence-related R&D support amounts to approximately $1 billion.[4] Other recent figures indicate that spending on science and technology, as broadly defined, accounts for approximately 1 per cent of GNP, or $4.0–4.5 billion for 1992, a portion of which might be devoted to military R&D.[5] In contrast, the US budget for military R&D is of the order of $50 billion a year.[6]

In the end, it is impossible to know with certainty the amount China spends on defence-related R&D. Spending on Chinese defence-related R&D may range in the vicinity of $1–2 billion annually but is

---

[4] See the section on China by David Shambaugh in Bergstrand, B.-G. *et al.*, 'World military expenditure', *SIPRI Yearbook 1994* (Oxford University Press: Oxford, 1994), chapter 12; and Arnett, E., 'Military technology: the case of China', in *SIPRI Yearbook 1995: Armaments, Disarmament and International Security* (Oxford University Press: Oxford, 1995), pp. 375–77.

[5] Figures derived from Humble, R. D., 'Science, technology, and China's defence industrial base', *Jane's Intelligence Review*, Jan. 1992, p. 4; *The Military Balance* (Brassey's: London, 1993), p. 152; and *International Financial Statistics* (International Monetary Fund: Washington, DC, Feb. 1994), p. 164.

[6] See the section on the United States in Bergstrand, B.-G. *et al.*, 'World military expenditure', *SIPRI Yearbook 1994* (note 4), table 12.8.

probably less. In any event, these figures suggest a relatively sparse Chinese investment in the technological future of its indigenous arms development and production programmes. Similarly, purchase or licence-production of large quantities of highly sophisticated weapons cannot be sustained by the Chinese economy at the moment. Alternative and less drastic measures are more likely, given the current economic resources available to the Chinese military.[7]

A second factor to consider is the impact of economic reforms on the ability of the Chinese defence production establishment to absorb and properly utilize weapons and technologies from abroad. It is unclear how deeply the economic reforms and diversification in the military production industry have affected its ability to maintain its production expertise and capacity. Official policy has maintained since 1986 the 16-character slogan on defence industrial policy which includes the assertions that 'military products have priority' (*junpin you xian*) and that the 'civil economy should support defence' (*yimin yang jun*). Beyond the rhetoric, however, it appears in some instances that the reforms centred on civilian production are eroding the capabilities of the Chinese defence industry to maintain production, let alone successfully integrate foreign weapon technologies. Numerous reports suggest that the Chinese defence sector has 'converted' as much as 70 per cent of its capacity from military to civilian production.[8] According to official estimates, China North Industries Group (NORINCO), the huge military production conglomerate, has 70 per cent of its industrial output in civilian use goods, and this figure will reach 85 per cent by 1995; the China State Shipbuilding Corporation devotes 85 per cent of its business to civilian goods and technology.[9] Just as the PLA overall faces corrupt influences as the economy turns towards the market, so too may the defence industry be weakened in the rush towards commercialization and consumerism. According to reports by prominent observers, China may currently utilize as little as 10 per cent of its arms-production capacity, a situation which may be attributed to both decreased domestic and foreign demand and the diversification of the sector into 'non-military' use.[10]

---

[7] Naoaki Usui, 'Financial woes limit Chinese arms buys', *Defense News*, 28 Feb.–6 Mar. 1994, p. 1.

[8] This figure is open to debate and interpretation. See, e.g., the comments by John Frankenstein in Mecham (note 3).

[9] 'China', *Asia–Pacific Defence Reporter*, Aug.–Sep. 1993, p. 25; and Cheung, T. M., 'Elusive ploughshares', *Far Eastern Economic Review*, 14 Oct. 1993, p. 70.

[10] 'Making a modern industry', *Jane's Defence Weekly*, 19 Feb. 1994, p. 28.

In addition, some close observers have noted that the Chinese military does not reinvest its commercial earnings in weapons and military technology acquisitions and development, but rather ploughs its profits back into its more lucrative non-military investments.[11] Wendy Frieman writes that, while economic reform policy has opened the door to a massive influx of Western technology, the vast majority of that technology goes into sectors which are indirectly related to military production.[12] Thus the technological capabilities of the defence sector as a whole may not fully benefit from the modernization and open-door policies unfolding in China.

Furthermore, the reforming economy has had an impact on the very professionals who engage in military R&D and production. The lucrative opportunities which await skilled minds may lure technological expertise away from the state-run military–industrial conglomerates to 'take the plunge' in the private economy or to move towards commercially attractive production. Wendy Frieman notes that the 'open door policy has also made a career in non-defense related science more attractive than it might have been in earlier periods' and, as a result, the 'military sector might still have some of the best, but it no longer has all of the best, of China's scientists'.[13] However, even in the 'non-military' sectors of industry from which technologies could be transferred for military use—such as commercial aerospace—the reforms are having a potentially demoralizing effect on trained professionals: Zhu Yuli, President of Aviation Industries of China (AVIC), has expressed concerns about keeping 10 000 engineers, technicians and designers 'energized and committed to aerospace' when more lucrative opportunities may await.[14] Furthermore, the fact that China has turned (once again) to Russian scientific expertise to support its military modernization would suggest that the reforms have been unable to generate and sustain a sufficient level of technological sophistication within its own pool of military scientists and technical experts.[15]

---

[11] Tyler, P., 'Chinese Army gets down to business', *International Herald Tribune*, 24 May 1994, p. 1.

[12] Frieman, W., 'China's defence industries', *Strategic Digest*, June 1993, p. 865, reprinted from *Pacific Review*, vol. 6, no. 1 (1993), pp. 51–62.

[13] Frieman (note 12), p. 865.

[14] Mecham, M., 'With many suitors, China seeks "equal partnership"', *Aviation Week & Space Technology*, 25 Oct. 1993, p. 23.

[15] Tai Ming Cheung wrote in mid-1993 that more than 1000 Russian defence scientists and technicians had taken part in military–industrial exchanges since 1991, that 300 Russian sci-

Technological and administrative factors

China is clearly making efforts to modernize its forces through imports of whole systems and through technology transfers. However, the vast majority of weapon platforms of the PLA continue to suffer from a lack of sophistication and long-term reliability, even in so-called 'new' systems. With 'science and technology' and 'national defence' taking third and fourth place, respectively, in the Deng-era Four Modernizations programme, the reforms of the 1980s and the rapid growth of the 1990s have only had limited success in improving Chinese military capabilities. As Paul Godwin and John Schulz argue, the hierarchy of the Four Modernizations recognized the fundamental priority of improvements in industrial, scientific and technological capabilities before advances could be expected in defence.[16] Following this logic, the technological development of China's defence production would be slow in the near term but would be strengthened in the long term, at least in theory.

This prioritization manifests itself in the technological capabilities of the defence industries. A review of some of the products of China's military manufacturing gives an indication of the technological problems. In the naval production sector, for example, modernization will rely heavily on a new generation of missile frigates of the Jianghu and Jiangwei classes. The armaments currently on these vessels are typically antiquated Chinese-developed systems (such as the ship-launched HY-2 Silkworm anti-ship missile and the HQ-61 surface-to-air missile) based on 1950s and 1960s Soviet designs. Most importantly, the vessels themselves are poorly constructed and often do not meet modern standards of seaworthiness, so that even a significant upgrade of the ships through fitting of foreign weapon systems might not affect the long-term survival of the vessel. According to one report, Thai recipients of these vessels determined them to be fit only for patrol work and coast guard duty.[17] On a visit to a Chinese Jianghu I frigate in 1990, a Western naval analyst observed:

entific experts have permanent positions with Chinese institutions and that scores more have been 'quietly recruited' by Beijing. Cheung, T. M., 'China's buying spree', *Far Eastern Economic Review*, 8 July 1993, p. 24.

[16] Godwin, P. and Schulz, J. J., 'Arming the dragon for the 21st century: China's defense modernization program', *Arms Control Today*, Dec. 1993, p. 3.

[17] Slade, S., 'Thailand's push to blue water', *Naval Forces*, no. 6 (1990), p. 77.

Design problems are exacerbated by exceptionally poor workmanship. When a supposedly watertight door was closed a ring of light between the door and its sealing was visible . . . Damage control facilities are virtually nonexistent, with no centralized damage control station . . . There were strong suggestions that damage control training plays little part in PLA Navy practice . . . Welding standards were extremely poor, with signs of premature failure much in evidence. The Chinese diesel engines are reported to be unreliable and to have great difficulty in reaching rated power.[18]

Onboard a recently commissioned Jianghu III frigate, another analyst noted:

the 'Jianghus' are primitively equipped frigates, representative of a level of Chinese shipbuilding experience consistent with vessels acquired from the former Soviet Union, which themselves were based largely on World War II German navy concepts. In many cases the standard of outfitting predates World War II . . . long-term survivability at sea is not one of the series' strong points.[19]

Similar serious criticisms have been levelled against the fleet of 17 Luda Class destroyers in China's inventory.[20] Reports also indicate problems integrating foreign technologies into China's new-generation destroyer, the Luhu Class: poor engineering resulted in ineffective use of the two General Electric LM2500 gas turbine engines which power the vessel, requiring a costly and time-consuming structural redesign of the ship's engine compartment.[21] Facing these problems, the Jianghu frigates, newly commissioned Jiangwei frigates (Jianghu derivates) and Luhu destroyers currently in production are to be the backbone of China's modernized fleet.

The Thai experience with Chinese armour, artillery and naval vessels also reflects the poor quality of these weapon systems. A Western military affairs correspondent inspected Chinese armour in the Thai inventory and found serious and widespread problems relating to poor-quality construction, the exceptionally inaccurate firing system,

[18] *International Naval Newsletter*, 3 Aug. 1990.

[19] Jacobs, G., 'PLAN's ASW frigate Siping', *Navy International*, Mar.–Apr. 1993, p. 69.

[20] Jacobs, G., 'Chinese navy destroyer Dalian', *Navy International*, Sep.–Oct. 1992, p. 263. Such reports contrast sharply with the glowing praise the Chinese press gave to the Hudong shipyard, where nearly all of China's frigates are built. See 'The Hudong shipyard: the cradle of corvettes', *Jiefangjun Bao*, 17 Feb. 1994, p. 1, in Foreign Broadcast Information Service, *Daily Report–China* (hereafter FBIS-CHI), 8 Mar. 1994, p. 41.

[21] 'Tight fit', *Far Eastern Economic Review*, 1 Apr. 1993, p. 9.

poor suspension and tracking, and severe problems with the engine train of the T-69 MBT. He wrote:

the Type 69 could not be considered an effective combat vehicle in the state in which it was presented. The Thai officers present were of the opinion that the combination of track, suspension and engine faults seriously impair the fighting value of the tank. The engine emits clouds of black smoke, creating a massive visual signature, and the vehicle is exceptionally difficult to maintain, has an unacceptably high breakdown rate and is difficult to repair.[22]

Thailand halted its import of Chinese land systems, citing the poor quality and workmanship of the power plant, fire-control system and tracks, and the inferior main gun on the T-69 tanks it received, while criticizing the barrel life of Chinese 130-mm Type 59-1 artillery guns. Thailand was also disappointed in the naval sector: the last two of six Chinese frigates built for Thailand will be delivered as hulls with German engines; the ships will be outfitted with Western electronics and weapon systems after delivery.[23] Problems such as these apparently plague the Chinese defence production sector.

It might be added that in the most recent use of Chinese weapons in major warfare—the 1991 Persian Gulf War—they fared poorly. While Chinese weapons were not used extensively by Iraq, those that were engaged against the US-led Coalition forces (armour and Silkworm missiles) were easily destroyed by superior technology.[24] It seems that Chinese arms and technology import strategies can make only limited gains in overcoming these very basic deficiencies in Chinese arms production.

Compounding these technological problems are administrative and managerial difficulties which undermine the effectiveness of Chinese weapon development and deployment. These problems have been well documented by Chinese and Western scholars: wasteful spending, lack of accountability, the protected status of defence industrial policy, the preponderance of ideological over economic considerations, and strict barriers of secrecy and autonomy between military

---

[22] Slade, S., 'Chinese armoured vehicles: you get what you pay for', *International Defense Review*, Jan. 1990, pp. 67–68.

[23] Cheung, T. M., 'Order arms', *Far Eastern Economic Review*, 4 Oct. 1990, p. 20. More detailed descriptions of the numerous qualitative problems that Thailand faced with imports of Chinese weaponry are presented in Saw, D., 'Thailand—paying a price for security', *Military Technology*, Dec. 1990, pp. 24–29; see also 'Chinese Navy shows its defects', *Jane's Defence Weekly*, 20 Aug. 1988, p. 295.

[24] Higgins, A., 'Arms failure alarms Peking', *The Independent*, 13 Mar. 1991, p. 5.

and civilian economies.[25] These problems remain and in some respects may be worsened by the reform policies of the past 15 years. In discussions with persons employed with the Commission on Science, Technology and Industry for National Defence (COSTIND), it becomes clear that the process of arms development and deployment—including threat assessment, technological assessments, cost analysis, mission-specific design, R&D applications, effective use of resources and, of special relevance for this report, choices of foreign components and inputs—remains inefficiently coordinated, still the victim of the lack of horizontality evident in bureaucracies everywhere but particularly acute in China. As a result, the end-products of the process are often poorly planned and inferior weapon systems, not to mention a wasteful drain on material and intellectual resources.

While concerned researchers and officials in China seem determined to streamline this process, they have met with only limited success. For the arms acquisition and deployment system in China, the shift from a command-style, largely autonomous economy-within-an-economy behemoth to a more integrated, pluralistic, consumer-oriented and efficient operation will be long and painful. Development of the ability of Chinese military planners to successfully select, integrate and deploy foreign technologies and weapons will be an equally difficult process.

Should such administrative problems move towards resolution, the Chinese military will still face another, perhaps even more difficult managerial headache which has to do with technology absorption by the Chinese defence industries and the Chinese soldier. A number of Chinese and Western studies indicate the problems which Chinese industries face in developing the proper 'assimilative capacities' to apply new technologies successfully to indigenous processes. In particular, the lack of information flow and technology diffusion, poorly coordinated labour and capital markets, and the low priority given to the importance of assimilation are often cited as some of China's greatest difficulties.[26]

The successful integration of more modern foreign weapons and technologies into the PLA will also depend on the capacity of the

---

[25] Latham, R. J., 'China's defense industrial policy', ed. R. H. Yang, *SCPS PLA Yearbook 1988/89* (Sun Yat-sen Center for Policy Studies: Kaohsiung, 1989), and references to PRC publications therein.

[26] See the studies presented in Leuenberger, T. (ed.), *From Technology Transfer to Technology Management in China* (Springer-Verlag: Berlin, 1990).

Chinese soldier to absorb and properly utilize new techniques and capabilities associated with weapons of the future. However, given the relatively small amounts of advanced foreign weapon systems presently deployed with the PLA, it is reasonable to assume that relatively few members of the military receive extensive training and experience with these foreign systems and technologies. Furthermore, while the absorptive capacity of the Chinese soldier will depend on improving his basic education and training, the PLA actually faces a much more difficult task: to introduce and integrate new and foreign ideas and techniques into Chinese cultural and societal norms and perceptions, which are resistant to notions of technology and modernity. One of the Chinese official exhortations employed to spur defence industry modernization—'face the world, face modernization, face the future' (*mianxiang shijie, mianxiang xiandaihua, mianxiang weilai*)—addresses a larger cultural antagonism regarding things foreign and has significant implications for China's abilities to absorb and utilize weapons and military technologies from abroad.

The technological and managerial difficulties specific to China are part of a related set of problems which scientists and experts in all the developing countries face and which limit China's capacity to integrate foreign weapons and technology into indigenous military-related R&D efforts: the brain drain, lack of adequate support and facilities, lack of communication and interaction, and the attraction of 'pure' research over applied research.[27]

Domestic politics

The arms import process takes place within the broader complexities of the Chinese political and decision-making hierarchy which contribute to shaping strategic thinking regarding foreign weapons. In considering the future directions of Chinese arms imports, it is necessary to identify the likely future role of influential decision makers and institutions—personalities and influence networks powerfully affect policy in arms imports just as in other parts of the Chinese decision-making structure.

[27] Katz, J. E., 'Factors affecting military scientific research in the Third World', ed. J. E. Katz, *The Implications of Third World Military Industrialization* (D. C. Heath: Lexington, Mass., 1986), pp. 297–98.

future foreign arms acquisitions will depend in part on the future political influence of different individuals and factions within the Chinese military bureaucracy decision-making hierarchy. A good illustration of this point is the past, current and likely future influence of Liu Huaqing. Broadly responsible for the modernization of the PLA, he has been active in overseeing the purchase of advanced weaponry, and his rise to prominence since the early 1980s coincides with the increasing levels of arms imports. His background as a technocrat and assistant to Nie Rongzhen (former head and powerful patron of COSTIND's predecessor organization, the Science and Technology Commission for National Defence) in the early development of China's defence industrial base also places his personal loyalties and interests squarely in favour of modernizing the military and military production. He also appears to have taken a personal interest in the acquisition of some systems and technologies from abroad.

One report suggests that he is personally interested in the possibilities of acquiring an aircraft-carrier and has appointed one of his associates, Vice-Admiral Li Jing, Deputy Chief of Staff of the PLA, to conduct discussions with Ukraine concerning the *Varyag*.[28] According to an article by a reporter from *Jiefang Ribao*, Liu directly ordered the formation in 1987 of a training class for future aircraft-carrier commanders.[29] Should the influence of Liu and his protégés outlast the demise of their patron, Deng Xiaoping, then military modernization—in part supported by arms imports—can be expected to continue at the current levels and perhaps even increase. Moreover, the continued influence of persons in Liu's camp would suggest that naval and air weapons and components, including those purchased from abroad, will receive priority. However, his connection to Deng, his advanced age and his reputation for reticence lead observers to speculate that Liu's influence will wane in a post-Deng power struggle.[30] In any event, his present political prominence stands out as an important factor determining the current and likely future emphasis on importing advanced air and sea defence capabilities and on rapid military modernization in general. Another possibly influential player for naval imports in the years ahead will be Major-General He Pengfei,

---

[28] 'China: Ukrainian nuclear aircraft carrier', *Intelligence Newsletter*, 15 July 1993, p. 7.

[29] 'From China, a hint it's seeking aircraft carrier', *International Herald Tribune*, 13–14 Feb. 1993, p. 4.

[30] Yan Kong, 'Institutional developments in China's Central Military Commission', *Jane's Intelligence Review*, Sep. 1993, p. 425.

who in mid-1994 was promoted to Deputy Commander of PLAN. He was formerly head of the PLA Equipment Bureau, involved with arms procurement for the PLA. His good connections and influence in the decision-making circles of the Chinese military are reinforced by the fact that he is the son of PLA Marshal and veteran of the 1930s Long March He Long.

The political position and clout of other persons and institutions will also affect arms and technology imports. In particular, the roles of Poly Technologies Corporation and COSTIND, both leading players in Chinese arms trade activities, bear closer scrutiny. Poly may be best known for its activities as an arms exporter, but it also acts to facilitate arms purchases from abroad. The President of Poly, Major-General He Ping, has also served as the head of the Equipment Bureau of the PLA General Staff Department. From his experience in these two positions, he appears well situated to influence arms import decisions to the benefit of both Poly, which would act as a middleman for arms import deals, and Chinese military modernization. His influence is reinforced by the fact that his father-in-law is the paramount leader Deng Xiaoping. Other influential leaders at Poly include its Executive Vice-President, Wang Xiaochao (son-in-law of General Yang Shangkun), and its Chairman, Wang Jun (son of the late political leader Wang Zhen).

COSTIND has for many years sought to inject a greater rationality and professionalism into arms procurement decision making, with mixed success. Its bureaucratic interest lies in improving Chinese defence and defence production capabilities. This interest is at times served by the pursuit of foreign weapons and technologies, although COSTIND appears to give greater support to developing indigenous production. The long-time head of COSTIND, General Ding Henggao, is at the ministerial level and is a member of the CCP Central Committee. According to Hong Kong sources, as part of a general effort to increase the military's role in national construction following the 14th CCP Congress in November 1992, Ding was selected as one of 10 generals allowed to attend and advise meetings of the Politburo as non-voting members.[31] Like his father-in-law, Marshal Nie Rongzhen, Ding is in a position to influence future foreign arms pro-

---

[31] British Broadcasting Corporation, *Summary of World Broadcasts: Far East*, FE/1571, 23 Dec. 1992, p. B2/6.

Table 5.3. Leading persons and institutions in arms procurement decision making in China and their interrelationships, as of 31 December 1994

Name	Institution	Comments
Ding Henggao	COSTIND	As Director of COSTIND, his responsibilities include coordination and implementation of arms procurement for the PLA; son-in-law of revolutionary hero and head of COSTIND predecessor organization, PLA Marshal Nie Rongzhen; Ding's wife, Nie Li, is Deputy Director of COSTIND
He Pengfei	PLAN	Appointed Deputy Commander of PLAN in 1994; previously head of the PLA Equipment Bureau under the GSD; son of revolutionary hero and PLA Marshal He Long
He Ping	Poly	President of Poly Technologies and PLA major general; served in the past as head of PLA Equipment Bureau under the GSD; son-in-law of Deng Xiaoping
Liu Huaqing	CMC Politburo	As a PLA General and Vice-Chairman of CMC, responsible for day-to-day work of the body; long-time protégé of Deng Xiaoping and widely recognized as a military modernizer with significant influence; member of CCP Politburo Standing Committee
Nie Li	COSTIND	Until 1994, Deputy Director of COSTIND, closely involved in day-to-day operations and planning for this body; daughter of revolutionary hero and head of COSTIND predecessor organization, PLA Marshal Nie Rongzhen; married to Ding Henggao, Director of COSTIND
Wang Jun	Poly	Formerly high-ranking official in CITIC, China's largest investment company with close ties to Poly Technologies; chairman of Poly Technologies; son of Wang Zhen, former PRC Vice-President and party elder
Wang Xiaochao	Poly	Executive Vice-President of Poly Technologies; son-in-law of former PRC President and influential military leader, Yang Shangkun
Zhang Wannian	GSD	Appointed PLA General and head of General Staff Department of the PLA in Oct. 1992; in his position he officially supervises the activities of the Equipment Bureau and Poly Technologies

Name	Institution	Comments
Zou Jiahua	SC Politburo	Vice-Premier of State Council and formerly minister of ordnance industry, minister of the machine-building and electronics industry, and vice-minister of the COSTIND predecessor organization

Acronyms: CITIC = China International Trust and Investment Corporation; CMC = Central Military Commission; COSTIND = Commission on Science, Technology and Industry for National Defence; GSD = General Staff Department of the PLA; PLAN = People's Liberation Army Navy; Poly = Poly Technologies Company; SC = State Council.

curement. Further adding to COSTIND's political clout is the influence of its former Deputy Director, Lieutenant-General Nie Li, the daughter of Marshal Nie and the wife of Ding Henggao.[32] Table 5.3 clarifies the rather complicated relationships of some of the principal persons and institutions involved in China's arms imports. In reality, the relationships and connections are often not clear-cut, with positions and titles meaning less than personal and family ties and influence networks among the key decision makers.

At a broader political level, there is a debate in China over the import of military systems which pits the consumers against the producers of military hardware in China. The consumers—the military in the field—tend to prefer more advanced technologies and weapon systems. This understandable preference often means looking abroad, given the disappointing state of indigenous weapon development. On the other hand, non-military bureaucrats and state-owned defence research and production facilities will probably see it as in their interests to maintain and improve the domestic capacity to produce weapons. The future political influence of representatives of these points of view will have a bearing on future arms imports, although some form of the current compromise—the time-honoured approach

[32] Ho Pin and Gao Xin, *Zhonggong Taizidang* [Chinese Communist Party princes] (Canada Mirror Books: Toronto, 1992), p. 479. An Oct. 1994 source states that Nie Li has resigned her COSTIND position to take a seat on the Standing Committee of the Eighth National People's Congress. See *Directory of P.R.C. Military Personalities* (US Consulate General Defense Liaison Office: Hong Kong, Oct. 1994), p. iii.

of some limited imports with an effort to integrate foreign technologies into advancing indigenous production—will likely predominate. In sum however, if professionalism and competence are to play a larger role in the future decision-making processes of the Chinese military and bureaucracy (and this is not a forgone conclusion), then it can be expected that current levels of foreign acquisitions will be maintained and perhaps increased.

III. The international environment

External developments and threat perceptions

The Chinese leadership has acknowledged that the maintenance of domestic and regional stability is the primary goal of Chinese grand strategy and national development. In maintaining this stability, the PLA has a critical role to play in confronting threats, both at home and along China's borders. In determining the directions in which Chinese arms procurement will probably move, it is necessary to consider Chinese threat perceptions and the means by which China could address these threats. With the decline in the near-term threat posed by the Soviet Union—now by Russia—and with changes in the regional power balance in East Asia, Chinese strategists have increasingly turned their attention to threats emanating from the east and south-east, especially from the sea. In addition, since the early 1980s there have been persistent efforts by Chinese military planners to shift from the traditional concepts of a land-based protracted People's War to embrace a more flexible, modernized capability to respond to limited conflicts along China's borders. In response to this change in thinking, Chinese arms procurement for the future, including weapons acquired from abroad, will probably focus on an air- and sea-defence capability.

However, at the same time China's growth, both militarily and economically, will raise suspicions and tensions in the minds of regional leaders; this will not be missed in Beijing and may contribute to the perception of a hostile external environment on the part of Chinese security analysts. This classic example of the security dilemma may provide the necessary encouragement to China's increased interest in foreign weapons and weapon technology. A brief review of China's external security environment will help clarify these points.

Retreating land-based threats?: Russia, India and Viet Nam

China's traditional land-based threats—those emanating from the Soviet Union/Russia, India and Viet Nam—are in abeyance at present. Moreover, China has engaged with these neighbours to reduce sources of tension along their land borders and to introduce CBMs into the bilateral relationships. These developments have been particularly remarkable in China's relations with Russia, which have built on Soviet President Gorbachev's pioneering visit in May 1989 and the April 1990 agreement between the two former antagonists to govern the reduction of troops along their common border. Since then, Sino-Russian negotiations have produced a number of bilateral commitments, including efforts to establish a demilitarized zone extending 100 km on both sides of their border, closer military-to-military ties, a five-year agreement governing military visits and the exchange of force level and doctrinal information, and an agreement in 1994 intended to reduce tensions and the likelihood of conflict between the two countries.[33] In September 1994, during the summit meeting in Moscow between Presidents Jiang Zemin and Boris Yeltsin, the two sides reached agreement not to be the first to use nuclear weapons against one another and not to target nuclear weapons on each other's territory.

Similarly, although not so dramatically, Sino-Indian and Sino-Vietnamese relations have also improved, making significant progress in the fields of border agreements and implementation of CBMs.[34] On the other hand, China's relations with its neighbours to the east and south-east—Japan, Taiwan, the Korean Peninsula and in the South China Sea—and with the United States are often problematic and uncertain.

---

[33] Tyler, P. E., 'China and Russia act to avoid conflicts', *International Herald Tribune*, 6 Dec. 1993, p. 6; 'Terms trip "very successful"', Foreign Broadcast Information Service, *Daily Report–Central Eurasia* (hereafter FBIS-SOV), 12 Nov. 1993, p. 17; 'China near Russian defense pact', *International Herald Tribune*, 9 Nov. 1993, p. 2; and Karniol, R., 'Treaty between China and Russia in sight', *Jane's Defence Weekly*, 18 Sep. 1993, p. 8.

[34] See Agreement between the Government of the Republic of India and the Government of the People's Republic of China on the Maintenance of Peace and Tranquility Along the Line of Actual Control in the India–China Border Areas, signed in Beijing on 7 Sep. 1993; and 'China and Vietnam sign border pact', *International Herald Tribune*, 20 Oct. 1993, p. 2.

Partners or rivals?: Japan, Taiwan and South Korea

North-East Asia has always held a high priority in China's economic and security agenda. The region includes two areas of potential conflict—the Korean Peninsula and Taiwan—and China's traditional rival, Japan. On the economic front, Japan, South Korea and Taiwan are not only economic powerhouses but also important sources of capital, technology and management skills for China's economic development.[35] China's relations with the three North-East Asian states have since the late 1970s been primarily informed by this economic imperative, which is also likely to lead these neighbours to emphasize a continued caution over possible conflicts in North-East Asia in the near future.

In Beijing's view, the disintegration of the USSR has been a mixed blessing for North-East Asian security: it resulted in a virtual evaporation of the Soviet threat to the region but opened up old rivalries and led to more independent behaviour by some states in the region. The reduced military presence of the USA and Russia, the growing regional clout of Japan and the lack of institutionalized CBMs among regional actors all contributed to a certain strategic uncertainty throughout the region in the early 1990s. The changing threat perceptions among North-East Asian states led to an extensive modernization of their air and naval assets to protect the sea lanes of communication (SLOC) and to compensate for the reduced US military presence.

Backed by their growing financial strength, Japan, South Korea and Taiwan have all embarked on major force modernization programmes focusing on air and naval assets at the expense of ground forces.[36] Japan's acquisition plan includes more Kongo Class destroyers and AWACS (E-767s) aircraft, as well as an additional F-15s and new submarines during the 1991–95 Mid-term Defence Programme.[37]

---

[35] Japan was China's largest trading partner in 1993 with a total trade volume of $39 billion. In the same year, Taiwan ($14 billion) and South Korea ($9 billion) were China's fourth and sixth largest trading partners, respectively. See China's official statistics in Foreign Broadcast Information Service, *Daily Report–China* (hereafter FBIS-CHI), 19 Jan. 1994, pp. 1–2. On the other hand, China's trade volume with ASEAN in 1993 was $7.5 billion. See *FBIS-CHI*, 28 Oct. 1994, p. 3.

[36] On arms procurement in the region, see Gill, B., 'Arms acquisitions in East Asia', *SIPRI Yearbook 1994* (note 4), pp. 551–62.

[37] Ebata, K., 'Japanese budget cut despite "destabilizing factors"', *Jane's Defence Weekly*, 9 Jan. 1993, p. 13. Japan's naval modernization is in part influenced by China's growing strategic reach. Shigeo Hiramatsu, 'Chinese Navy and the revival of "Sinocentrism"', *Shin*

Taiwan has contracted to purchase six Lafayette Class frigates from France and is building additional Perry Class and PFG-2 Class frigates. In addition to the 150 F-16s and the 60 Mirage 2000-5s that Taiwan secured in late 1992, the first squadron of the Ching-kuo fighters became operational on 27 December 1994.[38] Despite the continuing land threat from the north, South Korea has also expanded its naval and air power. It not only plans to acquire 120 F-16C/Ds (72 of which will be produced under licence in South Korea) but also intends to acquire 10 domestically built destroyers and nine German Type 209 submarines before 2000 and up to 10 indigenous KDX-2000 frigates.[39]

China will be hard pressed to match such regional trends in defence modernization and Chinese military planners are well aware that their North-East Asian neighbours' naval and air forces, although smaller in number than theirs, are relatively modernized and well trained. However, China's future military procurement will be informed by its own assessment of security-related developments in the region.

China will remain extremely sensitive to Taiwan-related developments and will carefully monitor activites that might militate against the eventual unification of Taiwan with mainland China. Amid growing trade and political dialogue across the Taiwan Strait, Taiwan independence looms large—the one circumstance most likely to lead to a PRC military move against Taiwan. Jiang Zemin's speech of 30 January 1995 did not renounce the use of force if necessary to reunify Taiwan with the mainland. However, in a change of tone from all previous PRC policy statements about Taiwan, he claimed that such force would not be used against Chinese compatriots, but rather 'against the schemes of foreign forces to interfere with China's reunification and to bring about the independence of Taiwan'.[40] Nevertheless, Chinese procurement of submarines and the development of

Boei Ronshu [Journal of national defence], vol. 20, no. 3 (Dec. 1992), pp. 16–37; and interviews, Japan Defence Agency, Tokyo, Dec. 1994.

[38] Hu Hsun, 'Building up the island bastion', *Jane's Defence Weekly*, 22 Jan. 1994, pp. 24–25; and Baum, J., 'Winged', *Far Eastern Economic Review*, 12 Jan. 1995, p. 21.

[39] Karniol, R., 'Acquiring a global viewpoint' and 'Effecting a shift in strategy', *Jane's Defence Weekly*, 5 Nov. 1994, pp. 18, 20 and 21–22; and Grazebrook, A. W., 'More regional naval growth', *Asia–Pacific Defence Reporter*, 1995, Annual Reference Edition (Dec. 1994–Jan. 1995), pp. 12–17.

[40] Jiang's speech is translated in 'President's speech on Taiwan reunification', British Broadcasting Company, *Summary of World Broadcasts: Far East*, FE/2215, 31 Jan. 1995, pp. G/1–G/4.

improved missiles should be seen as part of China's military response to developments on Taiwan.

Relations with South-East Asian nations

Members of the Association of South-East Asian Nations (ASEAN) are gearing to modernize their military assets to safeguard their maritime interests just at a time when China's expanding strategic horizon puts an emphasis on maritime resources, especially those in the South China Sea. Although an 'arms race' does not properly or comprehensively define the current dynamic of military modernization in the region,[41] fears of a Chinese military build-up—in addition to other factors—contributes to the region's search for improved defence capabilities.[42] As with its other neighbours, China may see these moves as justification for its military modernization.

China is the world's fifth largest oil producer although, because of its high domestic energy demand, it did not become a net importer of oil until 1994. The increasing cost of using inland energy also means that offshore oil and resources would become increasingly important for China's economic development in the future. In fact, some Chinese Government experts argue that the South China Sea could provide China with 'survival space' (*shengcun kongjian*). Pointing to China's growing energy shortage, they claim that: 'In terms of resources, the South China Sea holds reserves worth $1 trillion. Once Xinjiang has been developed this will be the sole area for replacement of resources, and it is a main fallback position for lebensraum for the Chinese people in the coming century'.[43] In short, there is a struggle for China's strategic space and economic resources. China has taken several firm steps to assert its claims in the region, including the promulgation in February 1992 of the Law of the People's Republic of China on its Territorial Waters and Contiguous Areas, joint oil exploration with a US company in contested water with full PLAN backup,

[41] Gill (note 35).

[42] On China's military intentions as viewed in the region, see Roy, D., 'Hegemon on the horizon?: China's threat to East Asian security', *International Security*, vol. 19, no. 1 (summer 1994), pp. 149–68; Shambaugh, D., 'Growing strong: China's challenge to Asian security', *Survival*, summer 1994, pp. 43–59; Richardson, M., 'Beijing's uneasy neighbors', *Asia–Pacific Defence Reporter*, Feb.–Mar. 1994, p. 20; Opall, B., 'U.S., allies fear Chinese buildup', *Defense News*, 26 Apr.–2 May 1993, p. 1; and Singh, P., 'Concern at the Chinese build-up', *Asian Defence Journal*, Feb. 1993, p. 88. See also papers from South China Sea Conference, American Enterprise Institute, Washington, DC, 7–9 Sep. 1994.

[43] 'Treacherous shoals', *Far Eastern Economic Review*, 13 Aug. 1992, p. 16.

the expansion of a 1-km airstrip on Woody Island (Yongxingdao) in the Paracel Island group, the occupation of two more islets in the South China Sea in 1992, and the occupation in early 1995 of reefs claimed by the Philippines.[44]

Seen from this perspective, the South China Sea issue seems to serve as the current leitmotif of China's naval modernization and the greater allocation of funds for the PLAN. There are several military steps that Beijing could take to enforce its claim over the disputed waters: one military measure would be to acquire an aircraft-carrier, but this option in the short to medium term is extremely difficult to consider seriously from financial, technological, political and doctrinal perspectives. Another stop-gap measure is the development of an air-refuelling capability, which China is known to have acquired from several sources. Yet it remains unclear whether China has operationally mastered this technique for force projection.[45] Related to China's moves in the South China Sea are its efforts to build possible basing facilities off the shores of Myanmar. This bilateral relationship presents another strong indication of China's interests in becoming a greater influence in the region.

All in all, the growing importance of such interests as offshore resources, SLOC, regional influence and the Spratly Islands in China's economic and political development points to the need to extend the PLA's strategic reach, especially its naval and air forces.

Coping with a global power in the region: the United States

China's post-Tiananmen US policy problem can be summed up in the question of how to deal with a nation that is vital to China's economic development but whose values—and in the eyes of some in Beijing, whose strategic ambitions—pose a major threat to the legitimacy and

[44] Chanda, N. *et al.*, 'Territorial imperative', *Far Eastern Economic Review*, 23 Feb. 1995, pp. 14–16; 'Philippines sends more troops to Spratly Islands', *International Herald Tribune*, 20 Feb. 1995, p. 4; *International Herald Tribune*, 19 June 1992; and Alialwi, D. M., 'The conflicting claims in the South China Sea', *Asian Defence Journal*, June 1992, pp. 6–19. The PLA reportedly deployed additional aircraft on Woody Island in early 1994. See *International Defense Review*, May 1994, p. 10.

[45] Kristof, N. D., 'China obtains technology to refuel jets in midair, extending its power', *International Herald Tribune*, 24 Aug. 1992; Slade, A., 'USA pushing to block UK sale to Chinese', *Jane's Defence Weekly*, 17 Sep. 1988, p. 603; and Ackerman, J. A. and Dunn, M. C., 'Chinese air power', *Air Force Magazine*, July 1993, p. 59.

survival of the Chinese regime.[46] With the collapse of the Soviet Union, the geostrategic rationale that had guided Sino-US relations since the 1970s evaporated; the compatibility of domestic political and social values and economic benefits became central to their bilateral relations.

Chinese leaders largely see the US threat as ideological rather than military, as the USA promotes 'peaceful evolution' away from Communist rule. Their examples of this might include US pressure for human rights and prison labour reform in China. Continuing allegations about China's unfair trade practices and about missile proliferation are viewed as manifestations of the USA's disrespect for China's growing international status. However, China sees growing indications that the USA poses more strategic problems as well. The sale of 150 F-16s and many other advanced weapon systems and technologies to Taiwan demonstrates US intervention in the unification process and is in Beijing's view a serious violation of the three joint communiqués on Sino-US relations that were reached in the 1970s and early 1980s. Reflecting their frosty bilateral relations, military contacts between the two sides have been minimal and were resumed only in November 1993. From that time until the end of 1994, the two sides gradually warmed up to one another in the military sphere (see appendix 3). Subsequent events in the relationship in 1995 returned to the more problematic pattern.

Chinese security planners see that a reduced US military presence in Asia provides China with an opportunity to expand its influence. As observed by several Asian security scholars, China no longer views the US presence as necessarily contributing to regional security and stability.[47] With the exception of the US forces in Japan—where China sees US forces as 'containing Japan'—US forces elsewhere in Asia are viewed by Beijing either as a source of instability, as in the case of the Korean Peninsula, or as an obstacle, as in the case of the South China Sea. The release by the Pentagon in February 1995 of a strategy report for East Asia—in which the USA among other points commits itself to halting its regional troop reductions and calls for the

[46] Xiaoxiong Yi argues that the Tiananmen Square crisis opened up a fundamental dilemma in China's US policy—i.e., how to balance autonomy and interdependence—and eventually led China to devise new strategies towards the USA. See his 'China's U.S. policy conundrum in the 1990s: balancing autonomy and interdependence', *Asian Survey*, vol. 34, no. 8 (Aug. 1994), pp. 675–91.

[47] See, e.g., Shambaugh (note 41).

further development of theatre missile defences with regional allies—was not warmly received in Beijing.[48]

The likelihood that the two sides will come to blows appears slight, but each seems already to have identified the other as a long-term security risk. At the very least, China's defence modernization is geared to safeguarding its growing regional interests from the extensive reach of a superpower.

Long-term strategy

The regional issues raised above, when combined with the three components of Chinese long-term strategy—territorial integrity, national unification and continued economic development—will require that the Chinese Navy and Air Force play an increasingly important role. These services will play a part in maintaining and perhaps enforcing Chinese claims of sovereignty over the Spratly Islands, in protecting vital shipping lanes and potentially rich energy-resource deposits in the South China Sea for the benefit of China's economic growth and, perhaps most crucially, in providing a credible deterrent against independence-minded forces on Taiwan. In addition, Chinese strategists maintain strong suspicions about the longer-term intentions of Japan. For the foreseeable future, those areas where China perceives a likely security threat will be along its coastal area and territorial waters, including those outlying islands to which China lays claim.

Sources of supply

While China may wish to procure advanced armaments from abroad, it will probably be prevented from acquiring the most advanced technologies because of sanctions or national security considerations invoked by potential suppliers. The United States is likely to maintain a freeze on arms and arms technology sales, at least in the near term. Any change in this policy will be gradual at most and will probably involve attempts to reinterpret current understandings around the fringe of dual-use technologies. Russia has also displayed a certain reluctance to part with sophisticated weapons and technologies. Since Russia shares a long border and an historically rocky relationship with

[48] *United States Security Strategy for the East Asia–Pacific Region* (Department of Defense, Office of International Security Affairs: Washington, DC, Feb. 1995).

China, its national security-policy decision makers must be aware of the possibility that such technologies and weapons could eventually be turned against Russia. Current reservations about providing China with technologies and production licences related to such sophisticated weapons as the MiG-31, the Su-35 and anti-missile defence systems result partially from this kind of concern. Negotiations in the mid-1990s to establish a follow-on organization to COCOM did not include China, which may mean that any future technology transfer control regime will be set up in a way that views China as a target of, rather than a participant in, non-proliferation measures. These considerations would suggest that China cannot expect easily to obtain the highly advanced military technologies held by the Western allies and Russia.

On the other hand, under pressure from their home industries and from China, and with the memories of June 1989 drifting further away in the collective memory, several Western suppliers have taken decisions which signal greater opportunities for weapon and technology transfers to China in the future. Some of these decisions include the concomitant policy not to arm Taiwan. Such decisions have also opened the door to greater civil trade between China and its West European trading partners. Italy is said to have reinterpreted its arms export legislation to allow it to export some military-related equipment to China, and other European suppliers are eager to enter the Chinese arms import market, although as of the end of 1994 government policies in Western Europe continued to prohibit arms transfers to China.[49]

In the USA, government policy on export regulations, including those covering potentially dual-use items and export credits for defence products, is coming under pressure from defence industries and sectors of government to liberalize, an effort which has met with some success.[50] Recent decisions taken by the Clinton Administration will allow for greater flexibility for defence exports, particularly when they are seen to be in the national economic interest. Invoking the economic rationale, then US Under-Secretary of Defense for Acquisi-

---

[49] 'France, Italy will emphasize civil sales to China', *Defense News*, 17–23 Jan. 1994, p. 6.

[50] See, e.g., Letter to Secretary of Defense Les Aspin from Aerospace Industries Association in *U.S.–Taiwan Economic Relations*, Joint hearing before the Subcommittees on Economic Policy, Trade and Environment and Asia and the Pacific of the Committee on Foreign Affairs, US House of Representatives, 103rd Congress (US Government Printing Office: Washington, DC, 1994), pp. 82–83.

tion and Technology John Deutch was quoted as saying that 'international cooperation in the development of next-generation weapons would enable US businesses to open new markets by offering advanced US technology'.[51] With regard to China in particular, by late 1994 some analysts advocated a return to the policies of the early to mid-1980s which allowed for the transfer of defensive weapons from the USA to China.[52]

In addition, the current economic and political instability and lack of coherence within Russian decision-making circles may leave arms manufacturers a freer hand to deal with China. However, even at the highest levels of Russian politics, there is support for increasing arms exports. In 1992, President Boris Yeltsin declared:

This arms trade is also an enforced necessity for us today. It is a source of foreign currency, which is currently in extremely short supply. It is also a condition for supporting the defense sectors . . . cuts in weapons production would be a severe blow to the plants producing them. This abrupt turnaround would inevitably lead to social problems and leave millions of people on the brink of unemployment. The arms trade would act like a shock absorber on this process.[53]

Difficulties and pressures such as these found in the USA and Russia are also present in other major weapon supplier states. These developments could mean that China will be able to gain access to Western and Russian weapons and technologies and that this access may expand in the years ahead.

IV. Future arms acquisitions from abroad

Given these factors influencing China's future arms imports, some conclusions can be offered as to possible future directions in Chinese foreign weapons and weapon technology acquisitions. However, it is extremely important to note from the outset that the systems described in this section represent a kind of 'wish list' for China. China's needs

[51] LeSueur, S. C., 'US likely will relax third-party export rules', *Defense News,* 28 Feb.–6 Mar. 1994, p. 1.

[52] See, e.g., Wilborn, T. L., *Security Cooperation with China: Analysis and a Proposal* (Strategic Studies Institute, US Army War College: Carlisle Barracks, Pa., 25 Nov. 1994), pp. 24–25.

[53] Quoted from 'Boris Yeltsin: Russia has no special secret policy regarding nuclear issues', in FBIS-SOV, 24 Feb. 1992, p. 37.

are extensive, even if principally concentrated in the areas of air and sea capabilities, and cannot be met overnight. In addition, China faces many financial, technical and political obstacles in its quest for military modernization through arms and technology imports. Thus this section suggests some possible directions for Chinese arms imports but does not suggest that these are necessarily near-term purchases.

China will focus largely on 'force multipliers' and technologies rather than the import of whole systems. The areas of principal interest will be in upgrading air and sea capabilities, including some force projection, patrol and reconnaissance capabilities, and air and sea defence. China will limit its off-the-shelf purchases and seek to procure whole systems in small quantities, preferring to develop an indigenous capacity to produce advanced weapons through technology transfers and offset agreements. Table 5.4 provides data and information on the likely future Chinese acquisitions of arms and arms technologies by weapon system.

Naval procurement

With Liu Huaqing's appointment as Commander-in-Chief of the Chinese Navy in 1982, and his subsequent rise to the Central Military Commission and the Politburo Standing Committee of the Chinese Communist Party, Chinese naval doctrine went through a significant change. Liu advocates the view that the sea is a 'strategic space' and hence the Navy a strategic asset worthy of development independent of the army. The development of a more effective and powerful navy has several dimensions, including the formation of well-armed fleets, maritime surveillance and patrol capabilities, and amphibious assault capabilities.[54] This complements the seaward-looking strategic view which has developed in China since the early to mid-1980s.

However, of the armed services, PLAN has suffered most from neglect over the past 40 years and is in dire need of modernization in virtually all areas of advanced weaponry and electronics. The shipbuilding industry is experienced in hull manufacture but continues to have troubles in workmanship and in the development of sufficiently reliable and powerful engines. Because the navy will play such an important role in future threat scenarios, the need to modernize is par-

[54] Zhang Yihong, 'China heads toward blue waters', *International Defense Review*, Nov. 1993, p. 879.

Table 5.4. Future Chinese requirements for foreign weapons and technologies, by weapon system

Weapon system	Description/technology sought
Aircraft	
A-5M attack aircraft	It was reported in early 1993 that designers of this aircraft were seeking improvements which may require foreign assistance, including radar-absorbent composites, in-flight refuelling, night-vision capabilities, more powerful electronic jammer system and laser-guided weapons
B-7 attack aircraft	Under development for PLAAF and PLAN for maritime attack role; programme delayed, perhaps in part because of need for foreign technologies for radar and avionics upgrades
Su-27 or other combat aircraft	China may be seeking to co-produce this aircraft or an indigenous version; Russian suppliers prefer direct off-the-shelf export over technology transfer; currently under negotiation
SH-5 maritime patrol and ASW bomber	PLAN currently operates *c.* 4 of these aircraft near Qingdao; improved ASW, avionics and surveillance capabilities may be sought from foreign suppliers
Super-7 fighter	Fighter is upgraded version of F-7M, intended for export; initial cooperation with Grumman before 1989; now seeking foreign partners to upgrade avionics, navigation and weapon systems; possible that GEC-Ferranti, GEC-Marconi and Alenia are being considered for future cooperation
J-10 fighter	PRC effort to design and produce advanced fighter aircraft by 2005; extremely ambitious programme will require foreign assistance; may be receiving Israeli assistance drawn from defunct Lavi programme
Y-8 transport aircraft	Development of an airborne early-warning version being undertaken, with possible assistance from GEC-Marconi and Israeli companies
Z-8 helicopter	This helicopter is based on the French Super Frelon helicopter, first developed in the 1960s; initial production of the aircraft approved after flight trials in 1989; expected to play maritime

Table 5.4 contd

Weapon system	Description/technology sought
	role in anti-submarine/anti-surface warfare, minelaying/minesweeping and surveillance; advanced technologies to perform these roles may be sought from foreign suppliers
Missiles	
PL-9 air-to-air and PL-9N surface-to-air missile	Development of this missile and its follow-ons to arm Chinese aircraft likely to include foreign assistance; discussion in past included integration of components from US Sparrow, British Sky Flash or Italian Aspide; reports indicate that Israel will assist in development of PL-9, using Python III technology
Air defence missiles	Since 1990 China has placed a strong emphasis on development of air defence systems; cooperation for the future may include assistance from Russia as part of purchase of SA-10 Grumble air defence system in 1992; reported but unconfirmed cooperation with Israel involving US Patriot technology would also contribute to development of future Chinese air defence systems; further purchase of air defence systems from Russia can be expected
Ballistic missiles	Reported but unconfirmed cooperation in development of ballistic and cruise missiles includes: work with Iran on M-7 (Project 8610) 180-km range missile and on 1000-km range M-18 missile; working with Pakistan on further development of M-11 and other short- to medium-range missiles
Naval systems	
Luhu Class destroyer	A new class of destroyer which is advanced by Chinese standards; production of the vessel expected to continue, and will probably require more advanced defence, communications and propulsion systems from foreign sources
Jianghu and Jiangwei Class frigates	Missile frigates will require substantial upgrading, particularly in advanced anti-air and anti-missile defence, communications and electronics

Weapon system	Description/technology sought
Kilo Class submarines	Delivery of 1 submarine in 1995; further transfers of at least 3 are expected; the deal may include technology transfer

Sources: Jane's All the World's Aircraft 1993–94 (Jane's Information Group: Coulsdon, Surrey, 1993); *Jane's Naval Weapons Systems* (Jane's Information Group: Coulsdon, Surrey, 1992); *Jane's Air-Launched Weapons* (Jane's Information Group: Coulsdon, Surrey, 1988); Reed, J., *Defence Exports: Current Concerns* (Jane's Information Group: Coulsdon, Surrey, Apr. 1993); 'China unveils plan for modern warplane', *International Herald Tribune,* 18 Jan. 1994, p. 4; and Fulghum, D. A., 'New Chinese fighter nears prototyping', *Aviation Week & Space Technology,* 13 Mar. 1995, pp. 26–27.

ticularly urgent and provides modernizers with ample justification to seek advanced systems and technologies from abroad.

The two new classes of *major surface combatants,* the Jiangwei frigate and Luhu Class destroyer, are in production in Chinese shipyards and will form the basis of an expanded and more modern Chinese fleet. As currently equipped, these vessels lack modernized communications and defence systems, areas in which foreign procurement is likely. *Naval air defence* to improve the survivability of the new Jiangwei frigates and Luhu destroyers is especially needed. French and Italian systems are likely to arm some of these vessels, and it appears that some derivatives from Israeli technology will also go into future Chinese naval air defence systems. China also requires a significant improvement of its anti-ship missile defence, now possessing outdated anti-missile and electronic systems which would be no match against modern sea-skimming missiles and anti-ship missiles equipped with electronic counter-countermeasure capabilities. The procurement of foreign technologies is a likely avenue to achieve improved capabilities in these areas.

Much attention has been given to the possible Chinese acquisition of an *aircraft-carrier,* but such a purchase, while in the PLA's longer-range plans, is unlikely in the near future. China purchased the Australian aircraft-carrier *Melbourne* for scrap in 1981 and negotiated in 1988 with the USA in a failed effort to purchase a World War II-vintage decommissioned aircraft-carrier.[55] It is believed that such purchases could assist Chinese military designers and engineers in the development of aircraft-carriers, which are important for China's future naval strategy. Negotiations with Russian and Ukrainian officials to purchase an aircraft-carrier have been put on hold, owing to such factors as cost, reliability and preparedness of the PLA. Preparations are under way to acquire an aircraft-carrier eventually, but the enormous amount of work which must come first—including training, logistic, doctrinal and strategic plans, weapons and fleet development, political and diplomatic manœuvring—suggest that it may be decades before one can be purchased and put into effective operation.

With regard to *submarines*, China is making an effort to develop a new class of vessel which will serve in patrol and attack roles. Its submarine technology is outdated, and it will have to turn to outside sources of technology to upgrade its fleet significantly. The Agosta Class submarine—which France has exported in the past to Pakistan—is reportedly a model for the new class of Chinese submarine. However, Chinese purchases of Kilo Class submarines from Russia, and their hopes eventually to produce this warship under licence, may mean that the new submarine programme is on hold.

Airborne and air defence capabilities

To assert itself effectively over greater ocean distances, and to deal with contingencies in distant border regions, the PLA recognizes the basic need to achieve *in-flight refuelling* capabilities. According to a study by the *International Defense Review* in August 1988, China did not at the time possess the capability to perform in-flight refuelling operations. A British company, Flight Refuelling, signed a Memorandum of Understanding with CATIC in 1986 under which Flight Refuelling was to provide 20 air-to-air refuelling systems similar to those used by the British Royal Air Force. The USA and Japan, acting through COCOM, were able to prevent this sale, but not before some initial visits were conducted by Chinese Air Force officials to the Flight Refuelling facility and the RAF squadron which operates British tanker aircraft.[56] Since then, China has begun to develop this

---

[55] 'Not only scrap', *Far Eastern Economic Review*, 17 Mar. 1988, p. 11.
[56] Slade, A., 'USA pushing to block UK sale to Chinese', *Jane's Defence Weekly*, 17 Sep. 1988, p. 603.

capability with the assistance of either Iran or Israel—or both. A possible configuration has the Y-8 or H-6 bomber acting as a tanker to refuel Chinese Q-5 or Su-27 aircraft. According to one report, China has set up a training base for aerial refuelling, at Zhanjiang, opposite Hainan Island. China is not likely to operationalize its refuelling capabilities for many years, and probably not until after the turn of the century.[57]

For several years, China has been interested in procuring *airborne early warning* technologies from abroad. The PLA made inquiries about AEW and maritime surveillance items in 1989, including studies initiated by CATIC and Thorn-EMI for installation of the Skymaster multi-role radar in the nose of Y-8 transports. Previously, Litton Canada tested systems for maritime surveillance and associated avionics with China in 1985.[58] China may seek assistance from British and Israeli firms to upgrade its transport aircraft into an airborne early warning and maritime surveillance role. The PLA is also looking to improve its *maritime patrol* and *anti-submarine warfare* capabilities. In this case, it appears that the PLA will rely in part on upgraded versions of the licence-built Z-9 and Z-8 helicopters, with improved endurance, power train, weapon systems, and radar and sonar components—items which may be purchased abroad. The Z-9 and Z-8 will equip both the Jiangwei frigate and Luhu destroyer and serve in an anti-submarine and maritime patrol capacity.

Another priority for the military in the years ahead is *rapid airborne mobility*, to combat any internal unrest and for deployment to troublespots on China's periphery. In the early 1990s, the PLA upgraded rapid deployment and airborne forces. Further advances in this direction will require improved logistical and transport capabilities, part of which can be met through foreign purchases, such as the Russian Il-76 medium- to long-range heavy transport aircraft. China is believed to have ordered 10 Il-76s, which are capable of carrying some 125 paratroopers or 40- to 50-tonne payloads across a range of about 5000 km in just over six hours. China will need more such transports to move more significant amounts of men and *matériel*, suggesting that further purchases are possible.

---

[57] Ackerman, J. A. and Dunn, M. C., 'Chinese air power', *Air Force Magazine*, July 1993, p. 59.
[58] 'China', *Air International*, July 1989, p. 2.

Air defence is another major priority, emphasized perhaps in reaction to the Persian Gulf War, in which dominance of the air proved to be a critical factor in the Coalition victory over Iraq. China has acquired Russian air defence systems and is negotiating to purchase more. In addition, it is believed to be working with Israel to develop further its own advanced air defence system.

In the area of *combat aircraft* such as fighter jets and ground attack aircraft, the future path is unclear, although modernization through imports is certainly needed. Before the Su-27 purchase and reports forecasting the Israel-assisted J-10 programme, the J-8II upgrade was considered to be the near-term answer to China's aircraft modernization needs. But, with increased Russian and Israeli cooperation on other aircraft projects, the J-8II programme may be on hold or destined for export. At present, around 100–120 J-8 aircraft of all types are deployed in China, all of which could be upgraded to current J-8II standard, and the J-8II is designed to accommodate even further avionics upgrades from foreign suppliers.[59] A decision to massproduce the J-8II was still pending in 1995 because of possible alternative modernization paths (e.g., imports and co-production with Russia) and the apparent lack of export orders from China's traditional customers, who find the aircraft too cumbersome and overly powerful for their needs.

A new generation of combat aircraft has been under consideration for some time but these programmes will require significant foreign inputs if they are to be successful. The B-7 strike aircraft programme (including modifications for a maritime strike capability), the Super-7 (made for export), the J-9 and J-10 programmes and the A-5 upgrade programme have all appeared as part of the Chinese aircraft modernization programme in recent years. It is clearly not possible for China to pursue significant development and modernization of all these systems simultaneously, and its prospects are clouded by the possibilities of Russian imports or co-production.

[59] On the J-8II see *Jane's All the World's Aircraft* (Jane's Information Group: Coulsdon, Surrey, 1993), p. 56; and Mama, H. P., 'China advances in combat aircraft', *Interavia/ Aerospace World*, Oct. 1992, p. 20.

Reports state that China may import Su-27, MiG-31 and/or Su-35 fighters from Russia or assemble these aircraft in Chinese factories in a deal which would include the purchase of technology relevant to the aircraft.[60] Discussions held in 1994 and 1995 by the authors with US military attachés in China and with executives of Russian arms production enterprises suggest that such deals were not complete and awaited further negotiation on financing and the level of technology and production rights involved in the transactions. Reports in 1994 and 1995 indicated that the J-10, with possible Israeli assistance, would be China's next-generation domestically produced fighter.

In sum, while China is certainly interested in working with foreign partners to develop and acquire complete platforms and technologies for new-generation combat aircraft, a clear approach has not appeared. The reasons for this indecision may be the high costs involved and a continuing debate between those interested in developing a capacity to produce a truly indigenous advanced combat aircraft and those who would prefer to accelerate the acquisition and deployment process either through off-the-shelf imports or licensed production or co-production deals.

A secondary but serious problem faced by Chinese aircraft modernization programmes is a lack of export orders to fund further improvements, particularly those involving advanced components from abroad. Neither the J-8II nor the Super-7 programme has export orders to help finance its development. Similarly, the K-8 jet trainer has been unsuccessful in finding markets beyond the two partners on the project, China and Pakistan, thus putting in jeopardy the long-term financial viability of the programme. Small numbers of the K-8 have been produced (some half a dozen were delivered to Pakistan in 1994), but mass production and international competitiveness are severely hampered by the apparently poor quality of the aircraft, resulting in particular from a lack of sophisticated engine technology.[61]

---

[60] '"Made in China" deal is forged for Su-27s', *Jane's Defence Review*, 6 May 1995, p. 3; Boey, D., 'Chinese may choose Su-35 over MiG-29', *Defense News*, 28 Mar.–3 Apr. 1994, p. 14; and 'China seeks MiG-31 co-production deal', *Interavia Air Letter*, 23 Oct. 1993, p. 5.

[61] Opall, B., 'Chinese tout trainers for global market', *Defense News*, 7–13 Mar. 1994, p. 16.

V. Conclusions

Persistent problems

From this survey of contemporary and likely future trends in Chinese arms and military technology imports, several conclusions may be drawn. These conclusions may be spelled out in terms of continuing challenges to China on the one hand and continuing regional concerns on the other.

1. It should be emphasized that a wide range of problems stand in the way of a Chinese military modernization strategy based on arms and technology imports. These problems include prohibitive cost, political and bureaucratic infighting, limited absorptive capacities, managerial and administrative roadblocks, and supplier controls. Paradoxically, some of these problems derive from or are exacerbated by the Deng-era reform and modernization programme, which is the foundation of China's comprehensive security strategy for the next century. While there is little doubt that China wishes to utilize foreign technologies and weapons to improve its military capabilities, it is limited in its ability to do so and must turn to alternative and ultimately less-than-perfect solutions for its modernization needs. This alternative will almost certainly resemble China's traditional approach of limited imports of whole systems, with the aim of developing and producing indigenous technologies and weapons. This strategy has met with some success in the past, but it has consistently contributed to maintaining a wide gap between Chinese weapon systems and other military capabilities and those of the Western allies and the Soviet Union/Russia.

2. This report suggests that Chinese arms and arms technology acquisitions from the West have been modest, sporadic and problematic. Most of China's arms imports have come from Russia and other non-Western suppliers such as Israel, Pakistan and Iran, which raises a question about the quality of these transfers. Only recently have foreign suppliers, particularly Israel and Russia, begun to provide China with relatively sophisticated weapons and technology; the bulk of China's arms imports in the past have been Soviet systems based on 1950s and 1960s technologies. Even in the case of Israel and Russia, it is unclear to what extent these countries are willing to part

with top-of-the-line systems and technologies. As a result, it can be concluded that the foreign weapons and technologies which China has managed to acquire have been, for the most part, second-rate.

As a result, it would appear that China can expect only limited success in its efforts to improve its military capabilities through the acquisition of foreign weapons and technologies. The gains that China makes in this area will be incremental and relatively slow in comparison to the pace of development which can be expected in Western and even Russian military technologies. Quick breakthroughs in military capabilities are more likely to come about as a result of direct foreign purchases—such as that of the Su-27—but these are likely to be relatively modest in quantity and quality and will contribute in only a limited way to the overall modernization of the Chinese military.

3. More profoundly, it is important to recognize the historically consistent nature of the difficulties China confronts in balancing its needs for military modernization against unwelcome reliance on foreign inputs. China faces many of the same debates and paradoxes today as it did in the late Qing Dynasty. Assessments by Paul Godwin and William Tow illustrate this point: 'China's interest in defence-related Western technology is a function of the failure of its own defence industries and research and development (R&D) facilities to develop follow-on weapons systems and defence technologies from those the USSR provided between 1950 and 1960'.[62] To this point add the comment by Tow that '[i]f Chinese leaders fail to achieve an admittedly difficult balance between traditional Sinocentric concerns and the strategic requirements for closing the military technology gap with foreign powers, the People's Republic of China (PRC) may eventually lose a large share of its geopolitical independence'. [63]

Written between 10 and 15 years ago, these two observations echo century-old problems and continue to ring true today. More recently, John Frankenstein summarized the resonance of history for present-day Chinese military modernization in terms of three continuing debates: the reformist open-door polices versus the struggle to uphold the Four Cardinal Principles and resist 'bourgeois liberalism'; the

---

[62] Godwin, P. H. B., 'China and the second world: the search for defense technology', *Contemporary China* (fall 1978), p. 3.

[63] Tow, W. T., 'Science and technology in China's defense', *Problems of Communism* (July–Aug. 1985), p. 15. Replace 'People's Republic of China' with 'China', and this statement is identical in essence to Feng Guifen's memorials on this same subject 150 years ago.

ideological struggle over the virtues of being a 'red' or an 'expert'; and the problem of balancing self-reliance with dependence.[64]

Of particular note, Chinese defence modernization may resist the trend of 'globalization' or 'internationalization' of military industries. This trend is already widespread among major arms producers, particularly in the West, and is likely to increase as defence manufacturers seek foreign partners as a means to access new technologies, spread R&D costs and guarantee future markets. It is also a trend which the closed Chinese defence modernization system and even more wary Chinese leadership is not likely to embrace quickly.

This analysis suggests the difficulties China has in reconciling domestic cultural and political forces with the strategic requirements of military modernization, including cooperation with foreign partners, and to translate that cooperation into a self-sufficient capacity to produce sophisticated weaponry at a technological level close to that of other major arms producers in the world. The powerful and continuing influence of the traditional *tiyong* concept—'Chinese learning for substance, Western learning for use'—has both sustained and hindered China's 150-year quest for military modernization. This will continue to have important implications for Chinese military power and influence in the years ahead.

Perceptions of China: stabilizing or destabilizing?

China's growing strategic presence in Asia—assisted in part by foreign arms acquisitions—raises questions as to China's future intentions. Many observers point with alarm to the potential for China to exercise its power in a forceful way in the South China Sea, engaging its neighbours in military conflict. This view is balanced by those who argue that China is unlikely to use overt force to seize its claims there, for fear of the potentially disastrous economic and political ramifications of such a move, and the Chinese Navy's continued inability to project power on a sustained basis.[65] A similar analysis applies to

[64] Frankenstein, J., 'The People's Republic of China: arms production, industrial strategy and problems of history', ed. H. Wulf, SIPRI, *Arms Industry Limited* (Oxford University Press: Oxford, 1993), p. 275.

[65] Caldwell, J., 'Not worth the price: why China is unlikely to fight for the Spratly Islands', *Armed Forces Journal International*, Feb. 1994, p. 20. See also Godwin, P. and Caldwell, J., 'PLA power projection: year 2000?', Paper presented at the Fifth Annual Conference on the People's Liberation Army, Staunton Hill, Va., June 1994.

other areas around China's periphery—Japan and Taiwan—where, in addition to the political and economic consequences, Chinese military planners must take account of the superior weapons and technologies in the arsenals of these potential adversaries. Arms imports can probably not contribute in a meaningful way to altering this scenario, at least not in the short to medium term.

Meanwhile, less noticed is the quiet but consistent expansion of Chinese political and economic influence with some of its neighbours along parts of China's periphery. If the import of weapons and technologies can make a significant contribution to improving Chinese power and prestige *vis-à-vis* its neighbours, it will augment an already formidable political and economic influence which Beijing maintains with, for instance, Laos, Myanmar and North Korea. However, that military power is more likely to be wielded subtly, as a less visible although real aspect of China's influence.

Thus China will continue to increase its regional influence as its comprehensive national power grows in the years ahead. However, it will probably hedge against any renewal of local conflicts in the near term, and may even take a constructive role in ensuring a stable environment conducive to its economic modernization; continued peace and prosperity in the region will require constructive contributions on the part of China. If the interpretation presented here proves correct, then the impact on international security of the improvement of Chinese military capability through arms imports is not likely to manifest itself in violent military disruptiveness, but rather in the gradual and steady expansion of Chinese power and influence in parts of East Asia around it. The challenge will be to integrate a rising China in a way commensurate with continued regional stability and prosperity.

Finally, the possible re-export by China of foreign-supplied weapon systems and technologies also raises international security concerns. For example, one report suggests that China will incorporate Patriot missile technology gained from Israel into designs of the SA-10 Grumble air defence system which Beijing has acquired from Russia and will in turn re-export improved missile systems to foreign clients.[66] Similarly, China's efforts in 1994 to export the B-7 strike aircraft to Iran may also have involved the re-export of technologies and know-how gained from US sources in the early development

[66] Fulghum, D. A., 'New missile threats drive EF-111 program', *Aviation Week & Space Technology*, 10 May 1993.

stages of this aircraft.[67] To give another example, China and Pakistan were believed to be cooperating in the deployment of CSS-2 missiles in Saudi Arabia and are known to be collaborating on the M-11 and other shorter-range missiles. However, it is difficult to confirm such reports and, moreover, China's relatively poor record in assimilating and deploying new weapons and technologies does not bode well for the possible re-export of such technologies to third parties.

Other systems present a far smaller threat to regional stability. Chinese tanks, artillery, ships and aircraft are typically sub-standard in construction and capability and pose little threat to the more sophisticated systems developed in the West. Furthermore, China's list of clients has been dwindling, with Beijing now appearing to have carved out a niche for itself to sell conventional weapon systems to states that might otherwise have a hard time finding arms suppliers— Iran, Myanmar and Pakistan being principal cases in point. These considerations suggest that the military capabilities of China's weapon clients will probably not be significantly improved through weapon and technology imports from China.

The current and future problems and prospects of Chinese arms acquisitions from abroad are not new; as this report shows they are reminiscent of the difficulties China faced more than 150 years ago in its efforts to regain its great-power status. The persistence of these problems over time suggest that, at their heart, they may have more to do with deeply ingrained culturally and historically determined attributes of China than with technical questions of access, development, absorption and application. If this is true, Chinese military modernization through arms and technology imports will continue to be a slow and painful process.

---

[67] Boey, D., 'Chinese firm seeks bomber sale in Iran', *Defense News*, 28 Mar.–3 Apr. 1994, p. 38.

Appendix 1. Chinese imports and licensed production of major conventional weapons, 1950–93[a]

Supplier or licenser	No. ordered	Weapon designation	Weapon description	Year of order/ licence	Year(s) of deliveries	No. delivered/ produced	Comments
Suppliers							
Canada	3	Challenger 601	Transport	(1985)	1986	3	For VIP transport
	2	Challenger 601	Transport	1988	1988–89	2	Deal worth $35m; for VIP transport
Egypt	(4)	MiG-21MF Fishbed	Fighter	(1978)	1978	(4)	Ex-Egyptian Air Force; for use in development of J-7 III (F-7 III) fighter; part of payment for 60–80 F-6 fighters for Egypt
	(2)	MiG-23MF Flogger	Fighter	1978	1978	(2)	Ex-Egyptian Air Force; for use in development of Chinese fighter; part of payment for 60–80 F-6 fighters for Egypt
	(2)	Su-20 Fitter C	Fighter/ground attack	(1978)	1978	(2)	Ex-Egyptian Air Force; for use in development of Chinese fighter; part of payment for 60–80 F-6 fighters for Egypt

Supplier or licenser	No. ordered	Weapon designation	Weapon description	Year of order/ licence	Year(s) of deliveries	No. delivered/ produced	Comments
	(1)	BMP-1	AIFV	(1977)	1977	(1)	Ex-Egyptian Army; reverse engineered as Type WZ-501
	(2)	T-62	Main battle tank	(1977)	1977	(2)	Ex-Egyptian Army; for use in development of Chinese tank
	(2)	SA-3 SAMS	SAM system	(1977)	1977	(2)	Ex-Egyptian Air Defence Command; for use in development of Chinese SAM system
	(1)	SA-6 SAMS	SAM system	(1977)	1977	(1)	Ex-Egyptian Air Defence Command; for use in development of Chinese SAM system
	(6)	AT-3 Sagger	Anti-tank missile	(1978)	1978	(6)	Ex-Egyptian Army; for use in development of Red Arrow 73 (HJ-73)
	..	SA-3 Goa	SAM	1977	1977		Ex-Egyptian Air Defence Command; for use in development of Chinese SAM
	..	SA-6 Gainful	SAM	1977	1977	(10)	Ex-Egyptian Air Defence Command; for use in development of Chinese SAM

No.	Weapon	Type	Order	Delivery	No.	Comments
(6)	SA-7 Grail	Portable SAM	(1977)	1977	(6)	Ex-Egyptian Army; for use in development of Chinese portable SAM
16	SA-321H Super Frelon	Helicopter	(1976)	1977–78	(16)	For Navy; Chinese designation Z-8
8	SA-342L Gazelle	Helicopter	1987	1988–89	(8)	For evaluation; deal worth $29.7m incl HOT missiles; deal incl Chinese involvement in development of EC-120 (P-120L) helicopter
1	AS-365N Dauphin II	Helicopter	1980	1982	1	Prior to licensed production; Chinese designation Z-9 Haitun
6	AS-332 Super Puma	Helicopter	(1984)	1985–86	(6)	For 1 Luhu Class and refit on 1 Luda Class destroyer; deal worth $91.5m incl missiles and radar
2	Crotale Naval Launcher	ShAM launcher	1986	1990	2	
..	Rasit E	Battlefield radar	1986	1986	(5)	For 1 Luhu Class and refit on 1 Luda Class destroyer; deal worth $91.5m incl Crotale Naval Modular launchers and radar
..	Crotale Naval	ShAM	1987	1990	(32)	
..	HOT 2	Anti-tank missile	1987	1988–89	(96)	For 8 SA-342L helicopters; part of deal worth $29.7m
4	Bo-105C	Helicopter	1976	1976–77	4	Option on 16 more not used; probably for civil use

France

Germany, FR

Supplier or licenser	No. ordered	Weapon designation	Weapon description	Year of order/ licence	Year(s) of deliveries	No. delivered/ produced	Comments
Italy	85	Aspide	Air-to air missile	1989	1990–91	(55)	For planned J-8 II (F-8 II) fighters; status of last 30 uncertain after J-8 II development stopped 1990
Russia[b]	6	Il-76M Candid B	Transport	1992	1992	6	Deal worth $200m paid in commodities (offsets 60%)
	4	Il-76M Candid B	Transport	1993	1993	4	Status uncertain; licensed production planned
	24	MiG-31 Foxhound	Fighter	1992			
	2	Su-27 Flanker	Fighter	1992	1992	2	Original order for 12 incl 2 Su-27UB trainer version reduced to 2 Su-27UBs
	1	Il-28 Beagle	Bomber	1992	1993	1	Ex-Russian Air Force; exchanged for canned fruit
	(1)	SA-10b SAMS	SAM system	1992	1993	(1)	For Su-27 and MiG-31 fighters
	..	AA-8 Aphid	Air-to-air missile	1992			
UK	(100)	SA-10 Grumble Watchman	SAM Surveillance radar	(1992)	1993	(100)	For 1 SA-10b SAM system
	..			(1986)	1987	(1)	
USA	6	CH-47D Chinook	Helicopter	1989			Deliveries suspended June 1989
	3	Citation II	Transport	(1981)	1982	3	For VIP transport
	2	L-100-30 Super Hercules	Transport	1987	1988	2	For China Air Cargo; offsets probable
	3	Learjet 35A	Transport	1986	1987	3	For geographical survey

2	Learjet 36A	Transport	(1985)	1987	2	Incl 1 with SLAR radar; for geographical survey
6	Bell-206B JetRanger III	Helicopter	1985	1985	6	
9	Bell-212	Helicopter	1979	1979	9	
24	S-70C	Helicopter	1984	1984–85	(24)	Deal worth $140m
2	AN/TPQ-37	Tracking radar	(1987)	1993	2	Deal worth $62m; embargoed 1989, but released 1993
USSR[b]						
..	An-2 Colt	Transport	(1954)	1954–56	(30)	Prior to licensed production
..	Be-6 Madge	Maritime patrol	(1955)	1956	(10)	For Navy
..	Il-10	Close support plane	(1949)	1950	(100)	Number uncertain
..	Il-12	Transport	(1951)	1952	(20)	Ex-Soviet Air Force; number uncertain
..	Il-14 Crate	Transport	(1953)	1954–55	(40)	Number uncertain
..	Il-18D Coot	Transport	(1968)	1968	(5)	Number uncertain
..	La-11	Fighter	(1949)	1950–51	(200)	Number uncertain
..	La-9	Fighter	(1949)	1950	(50)	Ex-Soviet Air Force; number uncertain
..	Li-2T	Transport	(1949)	1950–51	(50)	Number uncertain
(40)	Mi-1 Hare	Helicopter	(1953)	1954–55	(40)	Number uncertain
24	Mi-17 Hip H	Helicopter	1990	1990–91	(24)	
..	Mi-4 Hound A	Helicopter	(1955)	1956–57	(50)	Prior to licensed production; Chinese designation Z-5 (H-5)
..	MiG-15bis Fagot	Fighter	(1949)	1950–54	(1500)	Incl MiG-15 standard version; Chinese designation J-2 (F-2)
..	MiG-15UTI Midget	Fighter/trainer	(1949)	1951–52	(50)	Number uncertain
..	MiG-17F Fresco	Fighter	(1953)	1954–55	(300)	Number uncertain; prior to licensed production

Supplier or licenser	No. ordered	Weapon designation	Weapon description	Year of order/ licence	Year(s) of deliveries	No. delivered/ produced	Comments
	..	MiG-19S Farmer	Fighter	(1957)	1958–59	(100)	Prior to licensed production; number uncertain
	..	MiG-21F Fishbed	Fighter	(1961)	1961	(20)	Prior to licensed production; incl some assembled from kits
	40	MiG-29 Fulcrum	Fighter	1991			
	..	MiG-9	Fighter	(1949)	1950	(20)	Number uncertain
	12	Su-24 Fencer	Fighter/bomber	(1990)			
	24	Su-27 Flanker	Fighter	1991	1992	(24)	Deal worth $700m (offsets 40%); incl 4 Su-27UB trainer version
	2	Tu-16B Badger B	Bomber	1957	1959	2	Incl 1 assembled from kit; prior to planned licensed production; later copied as H-6 (B-6)
	(150)	Tu-2 Bat	Bomber	1949	1949–50	(150)	Ex-Soviet Air Force; Chinese designation Du-2
	(40)	Tu-4 Bull	Bomber	(1954)	1955	(40)	Ex-Soviet Air Force; Chinese designation Du-4
	(10)	Tu-4 Bull	Bomber	(1952)	1953	(10)	Ex-Soviet Air Force; Chinese designation Du-4
	..	Yak-11 Moose	Trainer	(1949)	1950	(50)	Number uncertain
	..	Yak-12M Creek	Light plane	(1952)	1953	(50)	Number uncertain
	..	Yak-17UTI	Jet trainer	(1950)	1950	(20)	
	..	Yak-18 Max	Trainer	1949	1950–53	(60)	Number uncertain; prior to licensed production as CJ-5

..	BM-13-16 132-mm	MRL	(1949)	1950–55	(600)	Ex-Soviet Army; number uncertain
..	BM-14-16 140-mm	MRL	(1955)	1955–59	(500)	Number uncertain
(500)	Il-28 Beagle	Bomber	(1952)	1954–58	(500)	Chinese designation H-5 (B-5); prior to licensed production
..	JS-2	Main battle tank	(1951)	1952–53	(500)	Ex-Soviet Army; number uncertain
..	PT-76	Light tank	(1954)	1956–59	(400)	Number uncertain
..	T-34/85	Main battle tank	(1949)	1950–54	(2500)	Ex-Soviet Army; number uncertain
..	T-54	Main battle tank	(1954)	1956–57	(500)	Number uncertain; prior to licensed production as Type 59
(4)	SA-2 SAMS	SAM system	(1957)	1959–60	(4)	Number uncertain; prior to licensed production as HQ-1
..	SS-C-2b CDS	Coast defence system	(1962)	1963	(4)	Number uncertain
..	AA-10 Alamo	Air-to-air missile	1991	1991–92	(144)	For 24 Su-27 fighters
..	AA-2 Atoll	Air-to-air missile	(1959)	1960	(100)	For Mig-21F fighters; number uncertain; later copied as PL-2
..	AA-8 Aphid	Air-to-air missile	1991	1991–92	(96)	For 24 Su-27 fighters
..	FROG-1	SSM	(1955)	1956–57	(50)	Number uncertain
2	R-1 Scunner	SSM	1956	1956	2	Copy of German V-2; for educational purposes
..	SA-2 Guideline	SAM	(1957)	1959–60	(48)	Number uncertain; prior to licensed production as HQ-1
14	SS-2 Sibling	SSM	1957	1957–59	(14)	Chinese designation DF-1; prior to licensed production
..	SS-C-2b Samlet	Coast defence missile	(1962)	1963	(24)	Number uncertain

Supplier or licenser	No. ordered	Weapon designation	Weapon description	Year of order/ licence	Year(s) of deliveries	No. delivered/ produced	Comments
	..	SS-N-2 Styx	ShShM	(1959)	1960–63	(100)	Number uncertain; prior to licensed production as HY-1
	6	Artillerist Class	Patrol craft	(1954)	1955	(6)	Ex-Soviet Navy
	4	Gordy Class	Destroyer	(1954)	1954–55	4	Ex-Soviet Navy
	(4)	Komar Class	Fast attack craft	(1965)	1965–67	(4)	Prior to Chinese production of improved version as Hegu Class
	6	Kronstadt Class	Patrol craft	(1955)	1955	6	Ex-Soviet Navy
	7	Osa I Class	Fast attack craft	(1964)	1965–68	(7)	Prior to Chinese production of improved version as Huangfen Class
	(70)	P-4 Class	Fast attack craft	(1951)	1952–53	(70)	Some possibly assembled in China
	4	Romeo Class	Submarine	(1959)	1960–61	(4)	Prior to licensed production
	8	S Class	Submarine	(1954)	1954–55	8	Ex-Soviet Navy
	2	SO-1 Class	Patrol craft	(1960)	1960	2	
	4	T-43 Class	Minesweeper	(1954)	1954–55	(4)	Prior to licensed production
	(2)	Whiskey Class	Submarine	(1954)	1956	(2)	Assembled in China; prior to licensed production
Licensers							
France	..	SA-321H Super Frelon	Helicopter	(1981)	1985–89	(3)	Chinese designation Z-8; incl several versions
	50	AS-365N Dauphin II	Helicopter	1980	1982–92	(50)	Chinese designation Z-9 Haitun; incl production for civil use

Supplier	No.	Weapon designation	Weapon description	1988	1992–93	No.	Comments
Israel	(30)	AS-365N Dauphin II	Helicopter			(2)	Chinese designation Z-9A-100 Haitun
	..	Python III	ShAM	(1989)	1990–93	(1 996)	Chinese designation PL-8H
	..	Python III	Air-to-air missile	1990	1990–93	(3 227)	Chinese designation PL-9
USSR[b]	(450)	An-2 Colt	Transport	(1956)	1957–89	(450)	Chinese designation Y-5 (C-5)
	(1 000)	Mi-4 Hound	Helicopter	1956	1958–79	(1 000)	Chinese designation Z-5 (H-5); incl production for civil use
	..	MiG-15UTI Midget	Fighter/trainer	1954	1956	(0)	
	(1 300)	MiG-17F Fresco	Fighter	(1954)	1956–60	(1 300)	Chinese designation J-4 (F-4)
	767	MiG-17PF Fresco	Fighter	(1955)	1956–59	(767)	Chinese designation J-5 (F-5)
	379	Yak-18 Max	Trainer	(1952)	1954–58	(379)	Chinese designation CJ-5 (PT-5); later developed to CJ-6A (PT-6)
	..	SA-2 SAMs	SAM system		1963–68	(19)	Number uncertain; Chinese designation HQ-1; later further developed as HQ-2 SAM system
	..	SA-2b Guideline	SAM	(1957)	1963–68	(550)	Number uncertain; Chinese designation HQ-1; later developed to HQ-2 SAM
	(10)	SS-2 Sibling	SSM	1957	1960–64	(10)	Part of Sino-Soviet New Defence Technical Accord of Oct. 1957; Chinese designation DF-1
	1	Golf Class	SSB	(1959)	1964	(1)	No SLBMs supplied; used as attack submarine
	14	Kronstadt Class	Patrol craft	(1954)	1956–57	(14)	
	(80)	P-6 Class	Fast attack craft	(1955)	1956–66	(80)	

Supplier or licenser	No. ordered	Weapon designation	Weapon description	Year of order/ licence	Year(s) of deliveries	No. delivered/ produced	Comments
	4	Riga Class	Frigate	(1954)	1958–59	(4)	Chinese designation Chengdu Class
	..	Romeo Class	Submarine	(1959)	1963–88	(84)	
	26	T-43 Class	Minesweeper	(1955)	1956–66	(26)	
	(19)	Whiskey Class	Submarine	(1954)	1958–64	(19)	

[a] This register lists major weapons on order or under delivery, or for which the licence was bought and production was under way or completed during the period 1950–93. 'Year(s) of deliveries' includes aggregates of all deliveries and licensed production since the beginning of the contract. Sources and methods for the data collection, and the conventions, abbreviations and acronyms used, are explained in annual editions of the *SIPRI Yearbook*. Entries are alphabetical, by supplier and licenser.

[b] Data for the USSR apply to the period 1950–91 and for Russia to the years 1992–93.

Source: The SIPRI arms trade database, 1994.

Appendix 2. Chronology of Sino-Soviet/Russian visits on security, military and arms transfer matters, 1989–June 1995

Date	Description of visit
1989	
February	Foreign Minister Eduard Shevardnadze to China for summit meeting preparation
May	President Mikhail Gorbachev to China for summit talks and normalization of Sino-Soviet ties
July	Vice-Premier Tian Jiyun to Soviet Union for discussions with Joint Commission on Science and Technology
November	Liu Guangzhi, Ministry of Foreign Affairs Deputy Chief in charge of USSR and East European Affairs, to Soviet Union for border talks
December	Minister of Foreign Economic Relations and Trade Li Lanqing to Soviet Union to discuss economic ties
1990	
March	Minister of Foreign Economic Relations Konstantin Katushev to China to hold discussions on terms of trade
April	Premier Li Peng, accompanied by PLA Deputy Chief of Staff General Xu Xin, to Soviet Union to discuss border agreements and troop reductions
June	Central Military Commission Vice-Chairman Liu Huaqing to Soviet Union for arms negotiations, including purchase of Su-27 fighters, accompanied by Deputy Director of COSTIND Major General Shen Rongjun, and Minister of Aeronautics and Astronautics Lin Zongtang
	Rear Admiral Vladimir Khuzhokov, Deputy Director of External Relations Directorate of Soviet Ministry of Defence, to China for border talks
September	Foreign Minister Eduard Shevardnadze to China for discussions on border issues
October	Major General Wen Guangchun to Moscow to hold discussions on expanding military-to-military exchanges

Date	Description of visit
	Deputy Minister of Aeronautics Industry Yuri Bardin and Deputy Prime Minister Igor Belousov to China to hold talks on Chinese weapon purchases, particularly fighter aircraft
1991	
March	Deputy Minister of Aeronautics Industry A. Geratchenko to China for air exhibition and arms talks
April	Foreign Minister Aleksandr Bessmertnikh to China for discussion on border issues and summit meeting preparation
May	Chinese Communist Party General Secretary and head of Central Military Commission Jiang Zemin to Soviet Union for summit talks
	Defence Minister Dmitri Yazov to China to finalize Su-27 deal, set up training for Chinese fighter pilots
June	Deputy Defence Minister Vladimir Arkhipov to China for continued arms sales discussions
August	PLA Chief of Staff Chi Haotian to Soviet Union for discussions of military-to-military exchanges
1992	
February	Commonwealth of Independent States (CIS) Chief of Staff S. Samsonov to China for arms talks, including assurances on deliveries in wake of collapse of Soviet Union
March	Minister of Foreign Economic Relations Pavel Aven to China for resumption of arms talks
	Foreign Minister Andrei Kozyrev to China for resumption of diplomatic ties
April	Head of General Logistics Department Zhao Nanqi to Russia for discussions of arms purchases
	Air Force Deputy Commander A. Malyukov to China to discuss air force personnel exchange
August	Defence Minister Qin Jiwei to Russia to discuss technology transfers and arms trade
	Vice-Premier Tian Jiyun to Russia for meeting of Joint Commission on Science and Technology
	Pacific Coastal Military Region Vice-Admiral A. Balusink to China to discuss provincial-level military cooperation
October	Deputy Defence Minister Andrei Kokoshin to China for talks on military conversion and air defence missiles

Date	Description of visit
November	Deputy Prime Minister Aleksandr Shokhin to China for talks on defence industrial cooperation
	Minister of Atomic Energy N. Mikhaylov to China for discussion on nuclear cooperation
	Foreign Minister Qian Qichen to Russia for summit meeting preparation
December	Russian President Boris Yeltsin to China for summit talks, including discussions on military cooperation and arms trade

1993

April	Navy Commander Zhang Lianzhong to Russia for talks on Kilo Class submarine purchase
May	Commander of Leningrad Military Region S. P. Seleznev to China for talks on provincial-level military cooperation
June	Deputy Naval Commander He Pengfei to Russia to continue discussions of Kilo Class submarine purchase
	Central Military Commission Vice-Chairman Liu Huaqing to Russia for arms talks, including discussions of possible tank purchase
July	Deputy Prime Minister Sergey Shakhrai to China to focus on economic issues
	Deputy Commander Igor Kasatonov to China for talks on expanded naval cooperation
August	PLA Chief of Staff Zhang Wannian to Russia to discuss details of military cooperation agreement
	CIS Vice-Admiral I. Khmelnov makes port visit to Qingdao
November	Defence Minister Pavel Grachev to China to finalize and sign military cooperation agreement

1994

January	Foreign Minister Andrei Kozyrev to China for talks on economic cooperation
April	Chief of Staff Mikhail Kolesnikov to China for arms talks and preparation for visit of Prime Minister
	Deputy Prime Minister Aleksandr Shokhin to China for talks on military technology transfers

Date	Description of visit
May	Prime Minister Viktor Chernomyrdin to China for talks on economic and border issues, including improvements in military relations, accompanied by Deputy Prime Minister Aleksandr Shokhin and Deputy Defence Minister Andrei Kokoshin
	Vice-Admiral Wang Jiying makes port visit to Vladivostok
June	Air Force Commander Cao Shuangming to Russia for talks on air force cooperation, including a show of interest in MiG-29 fighters
	Foreign Minister Qian Qichen to Russia for summit meeting preparation
	Deputy Prime Minister Aleksandr Shokhin to China for discussion of military conversion
July	Defence Minister Chi Haotian to Russia to finalize agreement on preventing dangerous military activities
September	President Jiang Zemin to Russia for summit talks, including discussions of military–technical matters; agreements reached on no-first-use and non-targeting of nuclear weapons against one another
November	Russian naval commander Felix Gromov to China to conclude Kilo Class submarine deal
1995	
May	President Jiang Zemin to Moscow to take part in 50th anniversary celebrations marking the end of World War II in Europe; meets President Boris Yeltsin to discuss bilateral relations
	Defence Minister Pavel Grachev to China to discuss reductions of troops and weapons on Sino-Russian border and military–technical issues
June	Premier Li Peng to Russia for discussions with President Boris Yeltsin and Prime Minister Viktor Chernomyrdin on bilateral relations and military–technical cooperation

Sources: Various issues of Foreign Broadcast Information Service, *Daily Report–China* and *Daily Report–Soviet Union/Central Eurasia.*

Appendix 3. Chronology of developments in Sino-US relations concerning military technology, June 1989–December 1994[a]

Date	Description of activity
1989	
June	In response to China's repression of Tiananmen Square protests, the US Government freezes arms transfers to China and halts high-level military-to-military meetings
October	Some 23 Chinese technicians working on the Peace Pearl Program at Grumman headquarters on Long Island, New York, and at Wright–Patterson Air Force Base in Dayton, Ohio, are authorized to return to work on the programme, after having been expelled from working on it on 7 June
December	Bush Administration approves the export of 3 communications satellites to be launched into space on Chinese launch vehicles; removes restrictions on US Export–Import Bank financing to US firms doing business with China imposed following Tiananmen crackdown
1990	
February	Citing national security concerns, US Government orders CATIC to divest itself of its ownership of a small US aircraft parts manufacturer, Mamco, which the Chinese state-owned enterprise had purchased in November 1989
1991	
May	US Government refuses to grant approval of export licence for US components to equip a Chinese domestic communications satellite; a Chinese state enterprise believed to be involved in the export of missiles to Pakistan was to receive the satellite components
	Owing in part to evidence that China had transferred ballistic missile technology to Pakistan, the US Government bars US companies from participating in Chinese satellite launches, and restricts the transfer of computer and missile technology to China; in addition, US companies are barred from selling technology and equipment to the China Precision Machinery Import Export Corporation (CPMIEC)

Date	Description of activity
1992	
February	Having received assurances that China would adhere to the guidelines of the Missile Technology Control Regime, the US Government lifts high-technology sanctions imposed against China in May 1991
December	Over the protests of the Defense Department and Arms Control and Disarmament Agency, the US Commerce Department approves the export of the AlliedSignal Garrett TFE731-2A-2A turbofan engine to China; the engine is to be produced under licence in China and will power the K-8 jet trainer; concern is voiced that the engine technology transferred could be used in Chinese cruise missiles; licensed production of engine is yet to begin in China as of 1995
1993	
January	In the closing days of his Administration, President Bush allows the export of Cray supercomputer to China, pending necessary processing
August	Citing evidence that 'items related to the M11 missiles have been transferred by China to Pakistan', the Clinton Administration bans US companies for 2 years from exporting items related to rockets and satellites to China or Pakistan, including a ban on dealing with 10 Chinese aerospace companies
October	US Assistant Secretary of Defense for Regional Security Affairs Charles Freeman visits Beijing, ending the ban on high-level military exchanges which the USA had imposed on China in response to the Tiananmen crisis
November	Clinton Administration agrees to allow the sale of generators and other components for China's nuclear power plants; announces the final go-ahead for sale of Cray supercomputer to China
1994	
January	Clinton Administration announces that commercial satellites under Department of Commerce auspices are not subject to August 1993 restrictions and that export licences for them could be approved
March	Discussions are held between Chinese and US counterparts to set up Joint Commission on Defense Conversion, for bilateral consultations on the conversion of Chinese and US arms industries from military to civilian use
May	In renewing MFN status for China, Clinton Administration maintains sanctions imposed in June 1989, including suspension of weapon deliveries, denial of licences for dual-use technology and suspension of consideration of licences for US Munitions List items

Date	Description of activity
August	Chinese Deputy Chief of PLA General Staff General Xu Huizi visits the USA and meets General John M. Shalikashvili, Chairman of the Joint Chiefs of Staff, and Defense Secretary William J. Perry to discuss the Sino-US military relationship; trip includes visits to Pacific Command headquarters and other major military installations in the USA; he is the highest-ranking Chinese military officer to visit USA since the Tiananmen crisis
October	US Secretary of Defense William J. Perry travels to Beijing to chair first official meeting of the Sino-US Joint Commission on Defense Conversion
November	Director of the Defense Intelligence Agency Lieutenant-General James R. Clapper, Jr visits China to discuss security and intelligence relations and tour Chinese military establishments

a On developments in Sino-US military technology relations from 1980 to 1988, see Tow, W. T., *Sino-Japanese–US Military Technology Relations* (Institute of Strategic and International Studies: Kuala Lumpur, 1988), appendix B.

Index